Bilston
C

Meanings into Words
Upper-Intermediate

Student's Book

Meanings into Words
Upper-Intermediate

An integrated course for students of English

Student's Book

Adrian Doff, Christopher Jones and Keith Mitchell

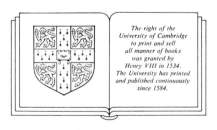

The right of the
University of Cambridge
to print and sell
all manner of books
was granted by
Henry VIII in 1534.
The University has printed
and published continuously
since 1584.

Cambridge University Press
Cambridge
New York   Port Chester
Melbourne   Sydney

Published by the Press Syndicate of the University of Cambridge
The Pitt Building, Trumpington Street, Cambridge CB2 1RP
40 West 20th Street, New York, NY 10011, USA
10 Stamford Road, Oakleigh, Melbourne 3166, Australia

© Cambridge University Press 1984

First published 1984
Tenth printing 1989

Printed in Great Britain
at the University Press, Cambridge

ISBN 0 521 28705 7 Student's Book
ISBN 0 521 28706 5 Teacher's Book
ISBN 0 521 28707 3 Workbook
ISBN 0 521 28708 1 Test Book
ISBN 0 521 24464 1 Cassette (Student's Book)
ISBN 0 521 24465 X Cassette (Drills)

KY

Contents

Introduction

This is the second of the two *Meanings into Words* Student's Books, which together take students from an intermediate level to the level of the Cambridge First Certificate Examination. It can be used after completing *Meanings into Words Intermediate*, or as an independent, self-contained course. *Meanings into Words Upper-Intermediate* can also be used by post-FCE students.

The Student's Book contains 15 teaching units, each of which is based on a major functional or notional area of English. Each unit includes:
– Presentation material which introduces key language items.
– Intensive controlled practice.
– Freer communicative practice and writing activities.
– An extended listening or reading activity.
– A Language Summary which lists the main points covered in the unit.

After each unit there is an Activities page. These activities give an opportunity to combine and extend the language learnt in earlier units and from *Meanings into Words Intermediate*. Unit 16 is a revision unit which contains free activities covering language from the whole *Meanings into Words* course.

Meanings into Words Upper-Intermediate Student's Book is accompanied by:
– A *Workbook* which contains extra written practice of the language taught in each unit.
– A *Test Book* which contains five Progress Tests and a Final Achievement Test.
– *Drills* (on cassette) which give intensive manipulation practice of key structures introduced in the units, and which are for use in the language laboratory.
– A *Teacher's Book*, which includes a general description of the course as well as detailed teaching notes on each unit.
– A *Cassette* of all recorded material in the Student's Book.

Thanks

The authors would like to give special thanks to David Jolly and David Scarbrough, whose wide-ranging ideas about communicative language learning have contributed much to the development of this course.

They would also like to thank the following people for their contributions to the recorded material: Carolyn Becket, Don Binney, Lucy Early and Sheena McDonald.

The authors and publishers would like to express their thanks and appreciation to the following institutions for their invaluable assistance in testing the course material and helping the authors to make many necessary improvements: The Bell College, Saffron Walden; The Bell School, Cambridge; The Bell School, Norwich; The Newnham Language Centre, Cambridge; The Studio School of English, Cambridge. Parts of the material have also been tested by the authors at the British Council, Beirut and Stevenson College, Edinburgh.

Unit 1   Experience

A

I studied French at university, and taught French in a grammar school for two years. I have visited most of the major European capitals, and have a good knowledge of German, Dutch and Italian, as well as French. Although I have never been directly involved in publishing, I have worked both as a translator and as a journalist

B

Martin Kingsley has written nine novels so far. Three of them have been best sellers, and have been translated into several languages. His fourth novel, **Out of the Blue,** won the Pulitzer Prize in 1969, and has been made into a film. He has also published two volumes of short stories. Mr Kingsley has travelled widely in the Far East, and has had first hand experience of the mental and physical hardships depicted in this novel.

C

Yes, it will be a lonely life, but I think I'll be able to cope. I've lived on my own before, and I'm quite used to looking after myself. I've lived in cold climates before, too. In Greenland, the temperature was often minus 40, or even lower, and that didn't do me any harm. I don't suppose you've ever

D

It took Kingsley several years to achieve any success as a writer. His first novel, *Eloise*, was rejected by no less than 15 publishers. He had to work in bars and restaurants to earn enough money to keep his wife and  two small children, and gave private lessons in French at weekends. He even considered giving up writing altogether

1 In paragraphs A, B and C, the writer uses mainly the Present Perfect tense. Why is this?
2 Sometimes the writer changes to the Past tense. Why is this?
3 In paragraph D, the writer uses *only* the Past tense. Why is this?

1.2 LISTING EXPERIENCES AND ACHIEVEMENTS

Practice

Look at 1.1 paragraph B again, and invent a list of experiences and/or achievements for each of the following:

1 She has had an amazingly successful film career . . .
2 The company has had one of the worst years in its history . . .
3 The escaped prisoner has an impressive criminal record . . .
4 The Colonel has had a remarkably adventurous life . . .
5 Jules' career as an anthropologist has taken him all over the world and into the most extraordinary situations . . .

Writing

Choose two of your answers and develop them into paragraphs. Begin with the sentences given.

1.3 HAVE YOU EVER . . .?

Presentation

You will hear three conversations in which people talk about experiences they have had. Listen to the tape and answer the questions.
1 What three questions do they ask?
2 What experience has each of them had?

Practice

Work in groups. Have similar conversations round your group, beginning with the remarks below:

1 They fined me for a parking offence last week.
2 They printed my picture in the newspaper once.
3 Somebody punched me on the nose this morning.
4 The customs men searched my luggage last time I came back from abroad.
5 Someone broke into my house two weeks ago.

Practice

You are asking two people about their leisure activities. One goes mountain-climbing, the other goes sailing. What questions could you ask them about their experiences?

Mountain-climber
a lot?
how many?
Alps?
highest mountain?
longest time?
most dangerous situation?
rescued?

Yachtsman
a lot?
open sea?
single-handed?
furthest?
longest time?
biggest yacht?
capsized?

Work in pairs. Interview the mountain-climber and the yachtsman.

Free practice

Choose one of your own leisure activities. In pairs, interview each other in the same way.

Presentation

THE PRICE OF SUCCESS?

Dawn and Rickie Handley, who shot to fame this month with their hit single 'Home Again', reveal what it feels like to be an overnight success.

DAWN: Well, there are a lot of things that we'll need to get used to professionally. We've always sung very informally – of course we've been invited to sing at social functions, like parties and weddings, and we've often had things written about us in the local press. But we've always sung mostly for fun, and we've never used any expensive equipment. And now suddenly it's all different – we sing in a studio, and we're told what to do by a producer, and we have everything recorded onto tape. I think it spoils it in some ways, but I suppose it's all part of being successful.

RICKIE: Yes, I think the biggest difference is going to be the publicity. We've always lived a very quiet life, and we don't usually go out much except to sing on Saturday nights down at the pub. But now all that's changing. We're already recognised in the street, and sometimes people stare at us or come up and ask us for our autograph, and we keep having our photograph taken. It seems really strange to us now, but I expect we'll get used to it eventually.

1 What things are Dawn and Rickie used to?
2 What things are they not used to?
3 Imagine other things that they will have to get used to now that they are famous.

Practice

The life-styles of the people below have just changed dramatically. In what ways are their lives different, and what kinds of problems will they have? Imagine what they are used to and what they are not used to.

She's just left her village and gone to work in the big city.

He's just retired.

They've just had a baby.

1.6 NEW EXPERIENCES Practice

Example: *I can't get to sleep . . .*
   . . . This is the first time I've ever slept in a tent.
   . . . I've never flown at night before.
   . . . I'm not used to having siestas.

   Now you've upset him. . .
   . . . It's the first time he's ever been spoken to like that.
   . . . Nobody's ever said 'No' to him before.
   . . . He's not used to being ignored.

Continue the remarks below in three different ways, as in the examples:

1 My feet are killing me . . .
2 God, this is embarrassing! . . .
3 Do you think you could slow down a little? . . .
4 She's feeling terribly nervous . . .
5 Hold my hand, will you? . . .
6 He's absolutely delighted . . .
7 I hope they get there all right . . .

5

1.7 JOBS   Free practice

1 Look at the jobs below, and choose the one that you think you could do best.

2 Work in pairs. Interview each other for the jobs you have chosen. Find out
   from the other person:
   a) how well qualified he/she is to do the job
   b) what relevant experience he/she has and hasn't had

   a cook   a shop assistant
   a decorator   a farm worker
   a film extra   a baby-sitter

1.8   APPLYING FOR A JOB

Reading

Read the letter of application below, and answer the questions.

```
                                              Mozartstrasse, 25
                                              Vienna
                                              Austria
         The Staff Manager
         Continental Tours Ltd
         6, Dover Street
         London W1                            11 March, 1983

         Dear Sir,
            I am an Austrian student, and am seeking some interesting form of
         employment for the summer vacation this year, and I have been advised to   10
         write to you to offer my services as a guide to British tourists visiting
         Europe.
            Briefly, my relevant experience and qualifications are as follows: I
         have studied English for ten years, first at school and since then at
         Vienna University. I have visited Britain several times, and in 1979 I      15
         spent ten weeks in the United States. My experience of speaking English is
         therefore quite considerable. I have also travelled extensively within
         Europe and have a good working knowledge of French and Italian in addition
         to my native language, German. My studies have included the History of
         European Art and Architecture as well as the languages I have just          20
         mentioned.
            I have worked as a tourist guide on two previous occasions and am
         familiar with the nature of the work. I have had to deal with many of the
         various problems and difficult situations that can arise during a tour –
         mistakes in hotel bookings, lost passports, illnesses, etc. Last summer I   25
         accompanied a party of Americans on a tour of Italy, and a month ago I
         acted as guide to a group of Irish businessmen visiting Vienna. I have
         always found this kind of work interesting and enjoyable and have had a
         good relationship with the clients who have been in my care.
            I look forward to hearing from you. Needless to say, I will be glad to    30
         supply you with any further information you may need, including references
         from my previous employers.
                                       Yours faithfully,

                                       Anton Mayerhofer

                               Anton Mayerhofer
```

1 The *main* reason that Anton gives for wanting the job is that:
  a) he needs the money
  b) someone advised him to apply
  c) he is interested in the work

2 Which languages does Anton know best?
  a) English and German
  b) French and Italian
  c) German and French

3 Write down *three* things that Anton is used to doing.

4 Explain in your own words the meaning of these expressions:
  a) 'I have also travelled extensively within Europe' (lines 17–18)
  b) 'a good working knowledge of French and Italian' (line 18)
  c) 'a good relationship with the clients who have been in my care' (lines 28–9)

5 a) How do you think Anton's studies of European art and architecture might be useful in the job?
  b) What kinds of 'mistakes in hotel bookings' (line 25) do you think occur?
  c) What problems, apart from those he mentions, do you think tourist guides often have to deal with?

Writing

1 You are going to write a letter of application for one of the jobs in 1.7 or any other job that you'd like to have. Choose the job you want, and make brief notes under these headings:

Name, age, occupation
Educational qualifications
Relevant experience

2 From your notes, write your letter of application.

Unit 1 Summary of language

In this unit, you have learnt how to:
– list experiences and achievements
– give details of experiences
– ask about experiences
– talk about familiar and unfamiliar experiences

KEY POINTS

1 *Present Perfect tense*
   I've work**ed** as a waiter.
   I've often **been** criticis**ed**.
   I've never **had** my handbag stolen.

2 *Present Perfect and Past tenses*
   I've studi**ed** engineering.
   I studi**ed** engineering while I was at university.

   – **Have you ever** been stopped by the police?
   – Yes I **have**. I **was** stopped last week while I was driving home from work.

3 *Special Present Perfect tense structures*
   What's the long**est** time you**'ve ever** spent alone?
   The most interesting country **I've ever** visited is Morocco.
   This is the first time I've (**ever**) had an article published.

4 *Be used to*
   He's quite **used to** spicy food.
   I'm not **used to** living on my own.
   She's not **used to being** laughed at.
   I'm used to having my photograph tak**en**.

Activities

FLATMATE

WANTED. Fifth person to share flat. Own room and use of kitchen, bathroom. 01-224 3532.
LOOKING for a flat? Room vacant, kitchen and bathroom shared. 336-7890.
ROOM VACANT in shared flat. Would suit single person. Use of kitchen. 221-0101.
EXTRA person wanted to share flat with four others. Own room, share kitchen. Male or female. 445-9872.

Students A, B, C and D: You are looking for a flat, sharing with other people but with your own room. You have seen the advertisements above in the newspaper, and you are going to visit each of the flats and meet the people already living there. You want to find out which flat would suit you best. Think what questions you will ask.

Groups 1, 2, 3 and 4: You are looking for an extra person to share your flat (with his/her own room), and you have put one of the advertisements above in the newspaper. People who have seen the advertisement are going to visit you. You want to find out which of them you would most like as a flatmate. Think what questions you will ask.

COMPOSITION

You are now living in one of the flats you visited. Write a letter to a friend, describing what it's like living there, and what the people there are like.

Unit 2 Appearance

2.1 JUDGING FROM APPEARANCES

Presentation

How do we use: 1 **look** . . . ?
2 **look like** . . . ?
3 **look as if/look as though** . . . ?

Practice

Look at the three pictures below. Make similar comments about them using the words given.

he needs a wash	terribly complicated	a honeymoon couple
rather aggressive	it cost a lot	they're celebrating
a tramp	very elegant	they're in love
angry	something from outer space	happy
he's going to start a fight	it gives excellent reproduction	they've just had some good news

2.2 LOOKS AS IF & LOOKS AS THOUGH   Practice

Example: You see a man lying on the ground in a pool of blood.

He looks	as if as though	he's just been shot. he's seriously wounded. he's in agony. he's about to die.

Talk about the people below in the same way. Talk about the past, the present and the future.

1 You see a girl standing on the seashore, staring into the water.
2 You see a man lying on the floor, laughing.
3 You see a woman whose clothes are soaked, and she's sneezing.
4 You see a man lying underneath a car.
5 You see someone climbing through a window.

Now try these:
6 You can hear people singing next door.
7 When you open the door of your flat, there's a strong smell of smoke.
8 When you touch your writing desk, you notice it's sticky.
9 When you drink a glass of water, you realise it certainly isn't ordinary drinking water.

2.3   GENERAL IMPRESSIONS: SEEM

Presentation

Mr Harvey's neighbours don't know him very well, but as far as they can tell . . .

. . . he's very friendly.
. . . he isn't very rich.
. . . he's happily married.
. . . he's some kind of businessman.

. . . he doesn't spend much time out of doors.
. . . he watches television a lot.
. . . he has lived a very interesting life.

1 Change each sentence using **seem**.
   Example He **seems** (**to be**) very friendly.
2 What do you think has led them to form these opinions?

Practice

Here are some things you have noticed about Mr Harvey. What do they suggest to you about him? Talk about him using **seem**.

He never stops to chat with you if you've got your dog with you.
His front garden always looks a bit neglected.
There are African masks on the wall of his sitting room.
The postman always delivers a lot of letters with foreign stamps to his house.
You only see his children during the school holidays.
He usually carries a walking stick when he goes out.

2.4   CAUGHT BY THE CAMERA   Free practice

Work in groups. Look at the photographs and talk about each one using **look** and **seem**.

1

2

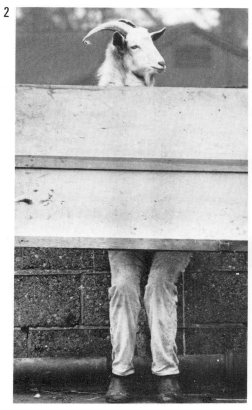

3

4

5

2.5 DESCRIBING PEOPLE

Presentation 🔲

You will hear a description of a man and a woman. Listen to the tape and:
1 Decide which of the six people in the pictures are being described.
2 Write the information you hear in the table below.

Hair	
Face	
Eyes	
Eyebrows	
Nose	
Lips	
Chin	
Special features	

3 Now write information in the table about the other four faces.
4 How can you ask and talk about:
   a) a person's complexion?
   b) a person's height?
   c) a person's build?

Practice

Work in pairs.
Student A: Think of a person in the class, and answer B's questions.
Student B: Guess who A has chosen by asking questions.

Example: A: What colour hair has she got?
             B: She's got blond hair.
             A: Is her hair wavy?
             B: No, she's got straight hair.
             A: Is she broad-shouldered?
             B: Yes, she is ...

2.6 GUESSING AGES   Presentation and practice

John was born between 1934 and 1936.

So he was born | **in the** thirties.
               | **in the** mid(dle) thirties.
               | some time **during the** thirties.

In 1953, he was **in his** late teens.
In 1960, he was **in his** mid(dle) twenties.
In 1967, he was **in his** early thirties.

Approximately how old is he now?

Say approximately when these people were born, and then decide
approximately what age they are now.
1 Richard 1930/3   4 Jane 1928/9
2 Alan 1964/5   5 Alison 1941/3
3 Susan 1895/1905   6 Geraldine 1960/61

Now work out these people's approximate ages:
1 Mike started school in 1947.
2 Albert Smith fought in the First World War.
3 Christine isn't quite old enough to vote yet.
4 Fred will be retiring in a couple of years' time.
5 My landlady doesn't look old, but she's got grandchildren.
6 Mary just remembers the end of the Second World War.
7 Brenda's been teaching for 25 years.

Look at the pictures in 2.5, and say approximately how old the six people look.

2.7 POLICE DESCRIPTION

Free practice

Here is the description of a man whom the police wish to interview in connection with this morning's £12,000 bank robbery in Leicester. The man is in his early thirties, is slightly built, and is about five feet eight inches tall. He has blue eyes and a pale complexion, and has shoulder-length dark hair. He is well-dressed, wears a gold ring and speaks with a London accent. Police believe he is still carrying the gun used in the robbery, and members of the public are warned not to approach him but instead to notify the police immediately.

Work in groups. Choose someone in the class (not in your group), and describe him/her. Talk about the person's face, general appearance, clothes and anything else that would help people to recognise him/her.

Writing

Write a 'police description' of the person you have chosen.

2.8 A STONY HOME

Listening

You will hear Lucy, a ten-year-old girl, talking about a picture by the Belgian surrealist painter, Magritte.
Listen to the tape and answer the questions.

1 Lucy uses the expression 'looks as though' twice near the beginning of the conversation. What exactly does she say?

2 Lucy suggests two possible explanations for the way the picture looks. What are they?

3 a) In general, how does she say she would paint the picture herself?
   b) How exactly does she say she would paint:
      i)   the bottle?
      ii) the book?
      iii) the outside?

4 a) How does Lucy describe the light in the picture?
   b) How does the interviewer describe it?

Discussion

1 Do you agree with Lucy that this is an interesting picture? Why/why not?
2 Why do you think the artist painted the picture in the way he did?
3 What title would you give to the picture?

Unit 2   Summary of language

In this unit you have learnt how to:
- talk about the appearance of people and things
- talk about your general impressions of people
- give precise physical descriptions of people
- talk about people's age

KEY POINTS

1 *Structures with 'look'*
   He **looks** ill.
   She **looks like** my sister.

   She **looks as** | **though** | she's enjoying herself.
                | **if** |

2 *Structures with 'seem'*
   He **seems** (**to be**) lonely.
   He **seems to be** a bachelor.
   They **don't seem to** eat very often.
   They **seem to have been** all over the world.

3 *Approximate age*
   He was born in **the** mid(dle) sixties.
   He's in **his** early twenties.

4 *Vocabulary*
   facial features
   general physical characteristics

Activities

THE I.Q. GAME

There is a kind of intelligence test in which people are given a common object and asked what different things it can be used for. The more variety in their answers, the better. For example, everyone knows that a brick can be used to build a house, but that's not all: what about keeping a door open, making a bookshelf, building a barbecue, writing, or even breaking windows?

You will hear ten uses of a common object, starting with the least familiar. After each one, try to guess what the object is (only one guess each time), and see how quickly you can guess the answer.

Work in groups.
1 Choose a common object and think of ten things you can do with it, including the obvious uses.
2 Number your answers from 1 to 10, starting with the least familiar and ending with the most familiar.
3 Form new groups. In turn, read out your ten uses, starting at number 1, and see how long it takes the others to guess what your object is.

COMPOSITION

Write 120–180 words on one of these topics:
1 Intelligence tests
2 Do-it-yourself
3 If you were shipwrecked alone on a desert island, which *five* common objects would you want to have with you? Why?

Unit 3   Relating past events

3.1   THE PAST PERFECT TENSE

Presentation

Read the passage below, which is the beginning of a novel, and answer the questions.

Julia Stretton was late. The Tartan Army had planted a bomb at Heathrow, and Julia, who had gone the long way round past the airport to avoid the usual congestion on the approach roads to the M3, had been delayed for two hours by police and army checkpoints. When she finally joined the motorway further down, she put thoughts of Paul Mason out of her mind, and concentrated on her driving. She drove quickly for an hour, breaking the speed limit all the way, and not particularly concerned about being spotted by one of the police helicopters.

She left the motorway near Basingstoke, and drove steadily down the main road towards Salisbury. The plain was grey and misty. It had been a cool, wet summer in Britain, and, although it was still only July, there had been reports of snow along the Yorkshire coast, and flooding in parts of Cornwall.

A few miles beyond Salisbury, on the road to Blandford Forum, Julia stopped at a roadside cafe for a cup of coffee, and as she sat at the plastic-topped table she had time at last for reflection.

It had been the surprise of seeing Paul Mason that had probably upset her more than anything else; that, and the way it had happened, and the place . . .

(Adapted from *A Dream of Wessex*)

1   In what order do you think the five events below happened?

Julia was stopped at army checkpoints.   Julia joined the motorway.
Julia stopped for coffee.   The Tartan Army planted a bomb.
Julia saw Paul Mason.

2   At which point in time does the writer choose to begin his story?

3   Complete these sentences:
   a)   Julia was late because . . .
   b)   According to the weather reports . . .
   c)   She was preoccupied because . . .

⋙→

Practice

The two series of events below are in chronological order. Join each series
together to make a paragraph, beginning with the sentences given.

1   Joan came home from work.
        She found Edward's note on the kitchen table.
        She quickly packed a suitcase.   When Edward arrived at the station,
        She took a taxi to the station.   Joan was already there. . .
    ▶Edward arrived at the station.
        Edward caught sight of her standing by the
          barrier.
        'Good,' he said. 'We're just in time.'

2   Most of Guy's friends left when the war broke
          out.
        Guy stayed.
        The war ended.
        Guy expected everything to go back to normal.
        The foreign companies stayed away.   Guy realised that the situation was
        Business didn't improve, and his money began   hopeless . . .
          to run out.
    ▶He realised that the situation was hopeless.
        Reluctantly, he made a decision.
        He picked up the phone and dialled the
          American Embassy.

3.2 PREVIOUS EVENTS   Practice

Example A: Her husband was horrified when she came back from the
             hairdresser's.

         B: Why? | What had happened?
                | What had they done?

         A: Well, they'd cut her hair really short, and they'd dyed it a kind of
            purple colour.

Work in pairs. Have similar conversations, beginning with these remarks:
1 When I saw him two years later, I could hardly recognise him.
2 They sent both men to prison for 20 years.
3 The fireman received a medal for bravery.
4 It was a good thing I checked my bill before I paid it.
5 When my sister came home, she was crying her eyes out.
6 I got a very angry letter from my bank manager last Monday.
7 My new trousers were ruined when they came out of the washing machine.
8 They came back from their holiday feeling completely refreshed.

3.3 PREVIOUS ACTIVITIES AND ACTIONS

Presentation

'I feel really exhausted. I've been working non-stop since seven o'clock this morning. I've been seeing customers all afternoon, and on top of that I've been to three meetings and I've dictated goodness knows how many letters. And I haven't eaten a thing all day.'

Complete what the speaker says a few days later:
'By the time I got home last Friday, I felt really exhausted . . .'

Practice

Example A: Sally was desperate.
B: She'd been drifting on the sea for five days . . .
C: . . . She'd used up all her water . . .
D: . . . She'd been trying to contact other boats on her radio . . .
E: . . . But nobody had replied to her SOS calls.

Work in groups. Talk about the people below in the same way.
1 Eventually Richard found a job that suited him.
2 When the Johnsons eventually got away on holiday, they felt they really deserved it.
3 By the time the climbers reached the top of the mountain, they were exhausted.
4 It was hardly surprising that Anthony fainted.
5 Vivienne sighed with relief.

Writing

Choose one of the five people above, and write a paragraph about him/her/them, beginning with the sentence given.

3.4 LOVE AT LAST   Free practice

The pictures and sentences below give the outline of a romantic story.
1 Decide what happened.
2 Write the story, incorporating the sentences given.

Barbara was glad the holiday was nearly over. What a bore it had been . . .

Of course, she had met André quite early on. But she hadn't stood a chance . . .

She decided to have a last swim before lunch . . .

When Barbara opened her eyes . . .

Barbara gazed into André's eyes. She could hardly believe . . .

3.5 ADDITIONAL INFORMATION: RELATIVE CLAUSES Presentation

They were really frightened now. Phil, (**1**), kept his foot pressed hard down on the accelerator, his hands tight on the wheel. Julia, (**2**), had started to cry. And Alex, (**3**), was grimly fingering his gun, (**4**). Only the dog, (**5**), seemed unconcerned. It wagged its tail as it looked back at the truck behind them, (**6**), . . .

Each of the sentences below could be incorporated into the passage as a relative clause.
Incorporate each of them in turn, as in the example.

Example (**1**) *Phil was driving.*
Phil, **who was driving**, kept his foot pressed hard down on the accelerator.

(**1**) Phil was an excellent driver.
Phil's forehead was covered in sweat.

(**2**) Julia hadn't wanted to come in the first place.
The Admiral had entrusted the papers to Julia.

(**3**) Alex had closed his eyes.
It had been Alex's idea to come.
The success of the whole mission depended on Alex.

(**4**) Alex had just taken the gun out of his pocket.
Alex never went anywhere without his gun.

(**5**) The dog was sitting facing the back window.
The dog loved travelling in fast cars.

(**6**) The truck was gaining on them all the time.
They were trying so desperately to escape from the truck.
A light machine gun was clearly visible on the truck.

Now read out the whole passage, choosing *one* relative clause for each space.

Read the story below and the additional information beside it.
1 Decide where each piece of additional information should be included.
2 Tell the whole story, incorporating the additional information as relative clauses.

Mary was woken suddenly by a strange noise. She sat up, startled. Then she froze, as she saw that the window was wide open. With a shock, she remembered that the servants had all left, and that she was all alone in the house. A floorboard creaked behind her. Turning, she saw an old woman. Suddenly, she realised who it was – it was her grandmother.

She had died exactly a year before.

She had laughed at them only that afternoon for being superstitious.

It seemed to come from outside her window.

She had been in a deep sleep.

Her mouth was twisted into a toothless grin.

She had locked it securely the night before.

She was dressed entirely in black.

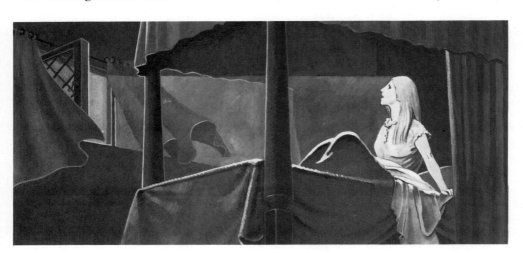

Now add an appropriate relative clause to these sentences:
1 I couldn't wait to get back to Venice, ...
2 At last they managed to repair the telephone, ...
3 The teacher, ..., turned round suddenly.
4 I eventually found the letter, ..., in my jacket pocket.
5 When I came back, I found that my car, ..., had disappeared.
6 We were all very grateful to Richard, ...

3.7   IT HAPPENED TO ME   Free practice

Work in groups. Tell the others about an occasion when:
either   you were very frightened
or   something exciting happened to you
or   something embarrassing happened to you
or   you were very lucky

3.8   A NIGHT TO REMEMBER   Listening

You will hear a story about Mr Wilkinson. Listen to the tape and answer the questions.

1   Which of these sentences about the story are true, and which are false?
   a) Mr and Mrs Wilkinson usually went to bed after 11.
   b) Mrs Wilkinson was woken up by a strange noise.
   c) The noise seemed to come from the garden.
   d) The noise was caused by the wind.
   e) When Mr Wilkinson went downstairs, his dog was in the dining room.
   f) Mr Wilkinson lay on the stretcher on his back.
   g) Mr Wilkinson broke his leg when he fell off the stretcher.

2   When Mr Wilkinson went downstairs, he acted very cautiously. Write down *three* things he did which show this.

3   What *three* injuries did Mr Wilkinson have by the end? What was the direct cause of each?

4   What two things did Mr Wilkinson need to do because of his excitement?

5   How did the ambulance men react when:
   a) they saw Mr Wilkinson's injuries?
   b) he told them how they had been caused?

6   Complete the sentences below, using the prompts given in brackets. Do them without listening, then check your answers on the tape.
   a) (light out / sleep) ... when Mrs Wilkinson heard a strange noise.
   b) The noise sounded ... (open / French window).
   c) Mr Wilkinson moved round the side of the room, so ... (not / seen / window).
   d) Meanwhile, Mr Wilkinson's dog, who ... (sleep / kitchen), ... (wake up / follow / dining room).
   e) Mrs Wilkinson cleaned the wound with cotton wool, which ... (throw / lavatory bowl / finish).

Unit 3   Summary of language

In this unit you have learnt how to:
– relate past situations to previous events
– talk about previous activities and actions
– give additional information in a story

KEY POINTS

1 *Past Perfect and Past Simple tenses*
When John **arrived** at the resort, the season **had** already **finished**. The weather **had** turned cold and wet, and most of the hotels **had** closed for the winter. He decided to drive on further south.

2 *Past Perfect Simple and Continuous tenses*
He **had been** walking all morning.
He **had** walked ten miles.
They **had been** camping for three days.
They **had** used up all their food.

3 *'Non-defining' Relative Clauses*
Anna, **who** had just woken up, was sitting in bed yawning.
Her car, **which** was ten years old, gave a lot of trouble.
I caught sight of Alan, **who**(m) I hadn't seen for years.
He went to see an old school friend, **whose** father was a lawyer.

The baby, | **who**(m) I'd been playing **with** quite happily | a moment before, | **with whom** I'd been playing quite happily |
suddenly burst into tears.

Activities

COMPUTERS: GOOD OR BAD?

(continued)

more popular. And so, for good or bad, computers are now part of our daily lives. With the price of a small home computer now as low as £50, experts predict that before long all schools and businesses and most families in the richer parts of the world will own a computer of some kind. Among the general public, computers arouse strong feelings – people either love them or hate them.

The computer-lovers talk about how useful computers can be in business, in education and in the home – apart from all the games, you can do your accounts on them, learn languages from them, write letters on them, use them to control your central heating, and in some places even do your shopping with them. Computers, they say, will also bring more leisure, as more and more unpleasant jobs are taken over by computerised robots.

The haters, on the other hand, argue that computers bring not leisure but unemployment. They worry, too, that people who spend all their time talking to computers will forget how to talk to each other. And anyway, they ask, what's wrong with going shopping, using pens and paper and typewriters, and learning languages in classrooms with real teachers? But their biggest fear is that computers may eventually take over from human beings altogether.

And so the arguments continue. Have you decided which side you're on?

⫸→

Work in pairs.

Pair A: You're a computer-lover. Your husband/wife is a computer-hater. You want to use some of your savings to get a home computer. Think of some arguments you could use to persuade him/her that it would be a good idea.

Pair B: You're a computer-hater. Your husband/wife is a computer-lover, and is interested in using some of your savings to get a home computer. Think of some arguments you could use to persuade him/her that it would not be a good idea.

Now form new pairs (one A and one B) and discuss whether to buy a home computer or not.

COMPOSITION

Write 120–180 words on one of these topics:

1 Write a letter to a newspaper saying how you feel about the growing use of computers in our daily lives.
2 What advantages and disadvantages do you think there are in using computers either (a) in business? or (b) in education? or (c) in the home?

SITUATIONS

1 You've just joined a multi-national class in a summer school. The teacher asks you to introduce yourself to the other students, and to say something about yourself. What do you say?
2 A friend says 'You were looking very angry when I saw you leaving work yesterday. What had happened?' Tell him/her.
3 Tell a friend what your impression of your teacher is.
4 You go skiing for the first time. Someone helps you get up after one of your falls. Thank him/her, and explain why you keep falling.
5 Someone asks you how well you know Germany. What do you say?
6 A friend of yours isn't quite sure whether he's met your brother/sister. Describe him/her briefly.
7 Someone asks you 'Have you ever been hurt in a fight?' What do you say?

Unit 4   Attitudes and reactions

You will hear three panellists on the radio programme 'Opinions' answering a
question put by a member of the studio audience. Listen to the tape and answer
the questions.

1 What do you think was the question put to the panel?
2 In general, what is the view of:
   a) Angela?
   b) Edward?
   c) Sheila?

3 Angela: 'I find television commercials extremely *annoying*.'
   What other words describing attitudes and feelings do the panellists use?
   How do they use each one?

4 Express each of the sentences below in *two* other ways.
   a) I find detective books boring.
   b) I'm amazed by some people's behaviour.
   c) Computers fascinate me.

Write the adjectival forms of the verbs below.

	Verb	Adjective
Examples	depress	depressing
	offend	offensive

impress............................   attract............................   upset............................

excite............................   irritate............................   surprise............................

interest............................   confuse............................   astonish............................

offend............................   shock............................   amuse............................

Work in groups. Talk about the people and things below, using an appropriate expression from the list.

Example: Politics

    A: What do you think of politics?
    B: Oh, I find politics really depressing.
    C: Yes, politics depresses me, too.
    D: Yes, I agree. I get terribly depressed when people talk about politics.

1 World Cup football
2 people who speak several languages
3 people who talk about themselves
4 people with dirty fingernails
5 slim people
6 horror films
7 people who swear
8 people who whistle all the time

4.3 YOUR OWN ATTITUDES

Free practice

Work in groups. What things in particular:

impress you?   embarrass you?
fascinate you?   terrify you?
offend you?   amuse you?

In your group discuss your attitudes to the following:
beggars
door-to-door salesmen
nudists

Writing

Write a paragraph about one of the topics you discussed.

4.4   IF THERE'S ONE THING ...

Presentation

Explain the difference between the relative clauses in these two sentences:
a) If there's one thing **that gets on my nerves** it's people who jump queues.
b) If there's one thing **I can't stand** it's people who don't look where they're going.

Now rewrite these sentences beginning 'If there's one thing ...':
1 People who smoke in restaurants annoy me.
2 People who are cruel to animals upset me.
3 People who break promises make me angry.
4 I hate people who smoke in restaurants.
5 I detest people who interrupt when I'm speaking.
6 I loathe people who ring me up early in the morning.

Practice

Example A: John got drunk again last night.

B: Huh. If there's one thing that | annoys me / I can't stand | it's people who | can't take their drink. / make an exhibition of themselves. |

Work in pairs. Have similar conversations, beginning with the remarks below.
B should *generalise* from the particular remark made by A.

1 Look. Fred's putting his cigarette out on his dinner plate.
2 Alice lost that book I lent her.
3 Jim drove into a lamp-post last week.
4 Rhoda still hasn't paid me back that £100 she owes me.
5 George has forgotten to feed the cat again.
6 Alma kept me waiting for more than an hour last night.
7 Mr Robinson came in to borrow some sugar again this morning.

4.5 THE WAY

Presentation and practice 📼

You will hear people in the street saying what they think of the British police.
Listen to the tape and answer the questions.

1 What different things do people like about the police?
2 What different things do people dislike about the police?

Below is a list of some typical characteristics of tourists. Make sentences
showing your attitude towards each of them.

Example: They make the streets so crowded.

I object to	
What I don't like about them is	**the way** they make the streets
The thing that annoys me about them is	so crowded.

They never bother to learn the local language.   They complain about everything all the time.
They spend so much money.   They help to provide employment.
They take up all the seats on buses.   They wear such funny clothes.
They take an interest in local customs.   They've always got so much energy.

Free practice

Work in groups.
Student A: You are a reporter. Interview the other people in your group. Ask them
             what they think of: (a) local TV programmes (b) doctors (c) the British.
The others: A reporter stops you in the street. Answer his/her questions.

34

4.6 REACTIONS Writing

Example: I was really impressed by that film ...

... I found the story very moving, and I liked the way they gave the atmosphere of nineteenth-century London so vividly. The acting was first-class and the background music suited the theme of the film very well. But the thing I found most impressive was the way the film managed to make you feel exactly what it was like to grow up in real poverty.

Choose three of the sentences below and develop them into paragraphs in which you describe your reactions.

1 I was very impressed by that restaurant ...
2 I found that TV documentary rather boring ...
3 I was extremely disappointed by his latest novel ...
4 I found that film absolutely disgusting ...
5 I thought the museum was really interesting ...
6 I found the circus quite exciting ...

4.7 JUDGING CHARACTER Practice

How would you describe a person who ...

... gives away lots of money?
... never buys you a drink?

... easily loses his temper?
... never loses his temper?

... helps other people?
... only thinks about himself?

... jokes about everything?
... doesn't joke about anything?

... expects good things to happen?
... expects bad things to happen?

... believes whatever you tell him?
... doubts what you tell him?

... worries about what people think?
... doesn't care what people think?

... likes going to parties?
... doesn't like going to parties?

... lets people down?
... doesn't let people down?

... has a high opinion of himself?
... doesn't boast?

'When I was ill last week, Mr Thomas next door brought me in all my meals, and posted my letters for me. And then when my car broke down yesterday he drove me all the way to the station in the pouring rain ...'

How would you describe Mr Thomas?

Work in groups. One student writes down one character adjective, and tells a story which illustrates it.
The others guess which word he/she has written down.

1. Which of the faces above do you find the most/least interesting? Why?

2. Imagine what the character of each of the people might be like.

3. To what extent can you judge people's characters from their faces? What other things can tell you what people's characters are like?

4.9 IT'S ALL RUBBISH REALLY

Reading

I have always found astrology a fascinating though rather silly idea. Somehow I can't believe that pieces of rock flying around in space should decide whether I'm intelligent or stupid, sociable or unsociable, generous or selfish. Astrologers say that our characters are influenced by the positions of the planets at the moment we are born. The Sun warms us, they argue, and helps things grow; the Moon causes the tides, and (according to some) can make people go mad. In the same way, say the astrologers, the planets and stars influence what we do, and the kind of people we are. I'm not convinced.

However, there's no doubt that astrology is still very popular. I'm always amazed at the way normally sensible people carefully read their horoscopes in newspapers and magazines. 'Of course, it's all rubbish, really,' they say, with an embarrassed smile on their faces, when they see you watching.

I'm the same myself. The other day I saw one of those Zodiac Star Guides in a station bookshop, and, of course, I put my hand in my pocket and took it away to read on the train – carefully hidden behind a newspaper. I'm a Gemini, and Geminis are supposed to be egotistical, so I turned straight to the Gemini pages and started reading about myself.

It began well. According to my Star Guide, I'm intellectual, quick thinking, imaginative, generous, charming, and everybody finds me extremely interesting to talk to. I also have a wide variety of interests, and am successful in everything I do. I began to feel sorry for the poor Taureans, who, according to the book, are rather boring, quiet, unimaginative people who never seem to do very much at all.

However, although all this was very enjoyable reading, it didn't impress me: it's easy to get people to believe nice things about themselves. But what about the faults? Will it get those too, I wondered as I read on.

It did. It seems that having a quick mind can have its disadvantages: besides being 'as changeable as the British weather', I'm rather quick-tempered, easily bored, and find it difficult to make decisions. Because of my many interests, the book continued, I can't concentrate on one thing at a time, and tend to be a 'Jack of all trades, and master of none'. More worrying was the discovery that I 'have no depth of feeling', and am unreliable in matters of love. And I was particularly upset to read that Geminis are sometimes not entirely honest.

By this time I was beginning to wonder whether the writer of the book was a personal acquaintance of mine. I was even (like a true, changeable Gemini) beginning to change my mind about astrology, and to stop feeling sorry for people born under Taurus.

But then I saw the trick: everyone has these faults, not just Geminis. We all sometimes lose our tempers, get bored, and change our minds – and nobody can be single-minded, serious, reliable and honest all the time. Slightly relieved, I put the Star Guide away and looked through the newspaper, stopping, as usual, to look at my horoscope for the day.

'Reading your horoscope?' asked the man sitting next to me.

'Yes,' I replied, with an embarrassed smile. 'Of course, it's all rubbish, really.'

1 According to the text:
   a) What is the main claim of astrologers?
   b) What argument do they use to support their claim?

2 a) Why do you think people might feel embarrassed about reading horoscopes?
   b) What *two* things did the writer do that show he feels the same way?

3 Explain the difference between (a) a horoscope and (b) the contents of the writer's Star Guide.

⟫→

4 Explain the meanings of these quotations from the writer's Star Guide:
   a) 'as changeable as the British weather' (lines 48–9)
   b) 'Jack of all trades, and master of none' (line 54)
   c) 'have no depth of feeling' (lines 52–6)

5 a) In the table, list the good and bad characteristics of Geminis given in the text.

Good points	Bad points

   b) What connections are there between the items in the 'good' column and those in the 'bad' column?

6 a) What effect did reading the good points have on (i) the writer's feelings? (ii) his attitudes to astrology?
   b) What about the bad points?

7 a) 'But then I saw the trick' (line 66). Explain what the writer thinks the trick is.
   b) How did the writer feel when he 'saw the trick'? Why?

Discussion

Work in groups.
1 Would you describe the writer as egotistical? Why/Why not?
2 What is your attitude to astrology? Is it 'all rubbish really', or not?
   What do you think of the arguments for and against astrology given in the text?
3 What are the good and bad characteristics associated with your sign of the zodiac?

Unit 4   Summary of language

In this unit you have learnt how to:
– express your attitude to people and things
– comment on people's characters
– describe your reactions to experiences

KEY POINTS

1   *Verbs and adjectives for expressing attitude*
People who complain a lot **depress** me.
I **find** detective stories excit**ing**.
I **find** people who spit in the street offen**sive**.
I **get** bored when people discuss money.
I**'m** impressed by people who've travelled a lot.

2   *Special expressions of attitude*
If there's one thing that depresses me **it's** people who complain a lot.
If there's one thing I can't stand **it's** people who shout.

I resent **the way** he keeps criticising me.
The thing that annoys me about him is **the way** he never says 'Hello'.
What I admire most about her is **the way** she always knows what to do.

3   *Reacting to past experiences*
I **was** very disappoint**ed** by that restaurant last night. The food wasn't very good at all.
The thing I disliked most was **the way** the waiters were in such a hurry – I **found** that really irritat**ing**.

4   *Vocabulary*
'character' adjectives

Activities

FILM STILLS

Work in groups.
Look at these film
stills and:
1 Make up a story
  that incorporates
  as many of them
  as possible.
2 Tell your story to
  another group.

COMPOSITION

In 120–180 words write

either the outline of the story you made up

or   a part of your story, incorporating at least two of the film stills.

Unit 5　Duration

Presentation　⬛

You will hear two dialogues. In each dialogue there are two questions with
'How long . . .?'
Listen to the tape, and then write the four questions and answers in the space
below.

Dialogue A　(He played cards.)

Q: How long ....

A: ....

(He drove his sister to Heathrow.)

Q: How long..

A: ....

Dialogue B　(She had to baby-sit.)

Q: How long..

A: ....

(She walked home.)

Q: How long ....

A: ....

Now answer these questions:
1　What is the difference between the two types of question with
　　'How long . . .'?
2　Explain the difference between　(a)　**for** and **until**
　　　　　　　　　　　　　　　　(b)　**in** and **by**

Practice

For each of the situations below:
a)　Ask a question with '**How long . . .**?'
b)　Answer it, using the words in brackets.

42

1 They talked on the telephone. (20 minutes)
2 She painted the bathroom ceiling. (six o'clock)
3 We played golf on Sunday. (dusk)
4 He mowed the lawn. (ten minutes)
5 I wrote all my letters. (lunchtime)
6 We had to change the wheel. (five minutes)
7 He watched television. (late movie came on)
8 I read the whole of *War and Peace*. (two weeks)
9 She did some piano practice. (bedtime)
10 She waited at the bus stop. (ages)

Now go through the situations again. Make sentences with **take** or **spend**.
Examples They **spent** 20 minutes talk**ing** on the telephone.
        It took her all afternoon **to** paint the bathroom ceiling.

5.2 YESTERDAY EVENING Practice

Work in pairs.
Listen to Dialogue A in 5.1 again and have similar conversations, based on these
situations:

1 A went to a discotheque.
  B had to write a report for his firm.

2 A went to visit an aunt in the country.
  B cooked a Chinese meal for some friends.

3 A rehearsed for a play.
  B went fishing and caught three salmon.

4 A repaired his car.
  B hitchhiked to London.

Presentation and practice

I ordered a taxi for ten to eight, but . . .

. . . it **didn't** come **for** half an hour.
. . . it **didn't** come **till** twenty past.

. . . **it was** half an hour **before** it came.
. . . **it was** twenty past **before** it came.

Complete these sentences in the same way:
1 I wrote to my mother by airmail, but in fact . . . (two weeks)
2 I intended to have an early night, but as it happened . . . (midnight)
3 I said he could borrow the record for a few days, but . . . (six weeks)
4 It was supposed to be a short meeting, but . . . (three hours)
5 She set us some homework for Monday, but as I was away for the weekend
   . . . (Tuesday)
6 He was invited to dinner, but, typically, . . . (after nine o'clock)
7 The job was supposed to take three weeks, but unfortunately . . . (nearly two
   months)

Practice

'We thought we would have no trouble finding a hotel room, but in fact most of
the hotels were booked up, because of the Music Festival, and it took us much
longer than we expected. None of the big hotels had any room, and it was
nearly midnight before we found a small hotel in the suburbs that had a vacant
room.'

Work in groups. Here are four things that took longer than expected. Imagine
why each one took so long, and what happened.
1 a train journey
2 writing a letter
3 a dental appointment
4 building a new motorway

Writing

Now choose one of the topics you discussed and write a paragraph about what
happened.

You will hear someone asking two people how long it takes to drive across
London. Listen to the tape and answer the questions.

1 What does the first person say it depends on?
2 What exactly does he say about
   a) the roads?
   b) the rush hour?
3 What does the second person say it depends on?
4 What exactly does she say about
   a) the best routes?
   b) one-way systems?
5 What advice does she give?

Work in threes.
Look at the questions below. What different things does each depend on?

How long does it take ... to get to New York?
                       ... to have your hair cut?
                       ... to get a university degree?
                       ... to learn English?

Now have similar conversations about each of the topics.

5.5 WORK AND HOLIDAYS   Free practice

Work in pairs.

Pair A: You are going to ask Pair B about their *holidays*.
         You want to find out:
         1 how long they spend doing different things
         2 how long it takes them to do different things
         3 about an occasion when something took longer than they expected
         Decide what questions you are going to ask.

Pair B: You are going to ask Pair A about their *work*.
         You want to find out:
         1 how long they spend doing different things
         2 how long it takes them to do different things
         3 about an occasion when something took longer than they expected
         Decide what questions you are going to ask.

Now conduct the interviews.

5.6 PAST, PRESENT AND FUTURE

Presentation

Here is part of a letter:

> We've been preparing for this trip for a long time. Bob went to Arabic classes for a couple of months, and I spent most of the summer reading all about the Pharaohs and ancient Egypt. We'll be staying in Egypt for about a month, so we'll need lots of luggage – we've been packing since last Tuesday, and we've still got lots more to do. We're planning to be back by Christmas, so what with the boat trip and everything, I suppose we'll be away for about two months altogether.

1 According to the letter, what time of year is it?
2 When will (or did) these activities *start* and *finish*?
   a) preparing for the trip
   b) going to Arabic classes
   c) reading about Egypt
   d) staying in Egypt
   e) packing
   f) being away

46

Practice

Look at the information about the two people below. Talk about the activities and their duration.

Paul is a painter. He started painting in 1970.
He went to Art School in 1973 and left in 1976.
He works in a studio in Amsterdam, which he bought just after leaving Art School.
At the moment he's painting a portrait of the Prime Minister, which he started two months ago.
Next week he's going on a three-month working holiday in Italy.

Vanessa starts training tomorrow for a tennis tournament that begins in two weeks' time.
This will be her tenth tournament. She played in her first one in 1980.
She spent part of the summer of 1975 (July and August) in California, where she first learnt to play tennis.
Last winter she took up squash, but after a couple of months she decided she didn't like it very much.
She's just signed a six-month contract to work as a tennis commentator on TV, and starts work later this year.

5.7 PERSONAL ENQUIRIES   Free practice

Work in groups.
Student A: You are *either* staying in Athens, on your way overland from
                                 Australia to England
                    or bored with your job and looking for a new one
                    or a TV personality
                    or yourself
The others: Ask A about his/her past and present life, and his/her future plans.

5.8 TOP DOGS

Listening 🖭

You will hear an interview with a dog-owner who lives in a high-rise block of flats. Listen to the interview and answer the questions below.

1 The council recently changed its long-standing rules about pets.
   a) What does *long-standing* mean?
   b) What change did the council make?

2 Which of these sentences are true and which are false?
   a) Mrs Compton's flat is very small.   c) She has three pets.
   b) She lives on the sixth floor.   d) She works all day.

3 She says looking after dogs is *time-consuming*, but *no bother*. What do these words mean?

4 Write down *four* things she has to do every day.

5 Give *two* reasons why it is especially important to house-train a dog if you live in a flat.

6 Here are two of the interviewer's questions. Complete Mrs Compton's replies:
   a) Interviewer: How long have you been interested in dogs?

   Mrs Compton: Well .... , I suppose,

   and ....

   ....

   b) Interviewer: I see, so it doesn't take very long to get them used to the idea?

   Mrs Compton: Well ....

   Sometimes you can ....

   but with the two I've got .... ,

   about six months altogether, I suppose.

7 a) What was the neighbours' attitude to her dogs when she first got them?
   b) Why did it change?
   c) How do the neighbours feel about keeping dogs now, and why?

Writing

Take notes from the speaker's account of how you house-train a puppy. Using your notes, and other information on the tape, write a short article for a magazine entitled 'Keeping a dog in a flat'. Use the outline below to help you.

1 training: (a) what you have to do (b) how long it takes
2 looking after your dog
3 advantages of having a dog

Unit 5   Summary of language

In this unit, you have learnt how to:
– say how long past activities lasted
– say how long it took to achieve things in the past
– say how long it takes to do things
– talk about duration up to now and in the future

KEY POINTS

1 *Past duration structures*
  How long did you stay at the party (**for**)?

  I stayed | **for** six hours.
           | **until** midnight.

  How long did it take you **to** get to the town centre?

  I got there | **in** an hour.
              | **by** ten o'clock.

  I spent the weekend sit**ting** in the garden.

2 *Structures for talking about the interval before an event*
  The film did**n't** begin **until** nine o'clock.

  It was | several days | **before** we got her letter.
            | Friday |

3 *Duration structures in different time periods*
  He studi**ed** French **for** three years.
  They**'ve been** mend**ing** the road **since** last Tuesday.
  I**'ll be** work**ing** in a bank **for** two months.

Activities

CARICATURES

Look at these photographs and cartoons.

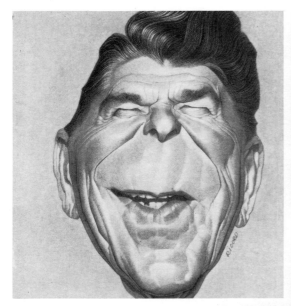

1 How are the cartoons different from the photographs?
  Which features of each person has the cartoonist exaggerated?
2 Why has he done this?
3 Write a short paragraph describing one of the two people.

COMPOSITION

Write 120–180 words on one of these topics.
1 Caricatures
2 Politicians
3 Can you tell what people's characters are like from their physical
  appearance?

Unit 6   Reporting

6.1   REPORTED SPEECH

Presentation

'. . . I met a really interesting guy last night. He was an Australian, and he told me he'd travelled to Britain for only £50: he'd worked his passage on a few boats, and then he'd hitchhiked through Europe. He said that since he'd arrived in London he'd been earning a living painting people's portraits in Trafalgar Square. He'd been an art student in Sydney, apparently. Anyway, he told me he was going to leave for America on Sunday, but he said he would come round and paint my portrait before he left . . .'

'The Minister said that the situation had certainly improved, although there was a long way to go before the Government achieved its targets. The rate of inflation had fallen, he said, to single figures, and was still falling, and he hoped that this would enable the Government to reduce the rate of income tax in the next Budget. The Minister stressed, however, that this depended on the cooperation of the Trade Unions. He was going to meet Union leaders later in the day, and said that he would announce the results of these discussions in Parliament.'

What do you think were the actual words spoken by:
1 the Australian?
2 the Minister?

Practice

Report these other remarks made by the Australian and the Minister.

Australian: 'I'm from Melbourne.'
　　　　　　'I like it here.'
　　　　　　'I don't earn much money.'
　　　　　　'I've got a cousin in America.'
　　　　　　'I'll be staying in New York for a month.'
　　　　　　'I'll go to Canada too if I have time.'
　　　　　　'I've been to all the art galleries in London.'
　　　　　　'I've been sleeping at a friend's flat.'

Minister: 'We're going to do all we can to help industry.'
'Unemployment figures have been falling for
several months.'
'The last government didn't do anything about
unemployment.'
'These proposals are being considered carefully.'
'Things won't get better unless we all work
together.'
'I fully support the Prime Minister's views.'
'I'm sure we'll win the next election.'
'I can't say any more until I've talked to the
Prime Minister.'

6.2 CONFLICTING REPORTS Practice

Complete the following:

1 I'm starving. I could eat a horse.
   But you told me just now . . .

2 Oh look. It's raining.
   What? But they said on the weather forecast . . .

3 The rent's £25 a week.
   But when I spoke to you earlier you said . . .

4 Can I have one of your cigarettes?
   But I thought . . .

5 Sorry. This is a private beach. Members only.
   But I was told . . .

6 I'd love to come, but I've got this essay to finish.
   What? I thought you said . . .

7 Didn't you get me a ticket?
   No, I didn't realise . . .

Work in groups.

Example A: I'll give you a lift in my car if you like.
            B: I didn't know you had a car.
            C: But you told me your car had broken down.
            D: But I thought your brother was using it today.

React to the remarks below in a similar way:
   I'm 25 today.
   I've got some lovely photos of Morocco.
   I hope you've brought a sleeping bag with you.
   Come on, or we'll miss the beginning of the film.
   When are you going to give me that book back?

Now continue with remarks of your own.

6.3 FORTUNE-TELLING   Free practice

Work in groups.

Student A: You are the fortune-teller. Sit apart from the others.
Tell the fortunes of the other people in the group one by one. Tell them about:
a) the kind of people they are
b) their past life
c) their future

The others: In turn, go to the fortune-teller and have your fortune told. When the fortune-teller has finished, go back and tell the others what he/she told you.

6.4   KINDS OF STATEMENT

Presentation and practice

You will hear part of a radio programme called 'Safeguard'. Listen to the tape, and answer the questions.

1 What is the purpose of the radio programme 'Safeguard'?
2 On what conditions did Mr Lock agree to order the drill?
3 For what two reasons did he send it back?
4 What did (a) Mr Lock (b) Bargain Electrics think should happen?
5 What happened after Mr Lock phoned Safeguard?

Listen to the tape again. Choosing appropriate verbs from the list, report the remarks below. Begin with the words given.

admit	explain	assure
deny	point out	insist
accuse	claim	warn

1 'You're under no obligation to buy the drill if you don't like it.'
The salesman . . .

2 'I don't want the drill, because it doesn't work.'
Mr Lock . . .

3 'The same drill can be bought locally for £10 less.'
Mr Lock . . .

4 'You broke the drill by using it wrongly, and you still owe us £45.'
Bargain Electrics . . .

5 'I did not break the drill.'
Mr Lock . . .

6 'The drill reached you in perfect condition.'
The Managing Director . . .

7 'If you do not pay the balance within seven days, we will have to take legal action.'
The Managing Director . . .

8 'You are interfering in a private matter.'
The Sales Manager . . .

9 'Mr Lock has been right all along – the drill was wrongly assembled in the factory.'
The Managing Director . . .

Practice

Work in pairs.
Student A: You are Mr Lock. A reporter from a local newspaper is interviewing you about your experience. Answer his questions.
Student B: You are a reporter on a local newspaper. Interview Mr Lock about his experience.

6.5 INFLUENCING AND TAKING ACTION   Presentation and practice

Here are some other remarks made by various people in the dispute over Mr Lock's drill. In each case:

a) decide who you think made the remark
b) report the remark, using a suitable verb from the list

agree	promise	advise	try to persuade
refuse	threaten	recommend	urge
insist		suggest	beg

1 'Come on, Mr Lock. Why not buy it? It's only £60, after all. Go on, it's an investment.'
2 'No, I have absolutely no intention of sending you the money.'
3 'If you don't pay up, we'll take legal action.'
4 'Frankly, I think you're asking for trouble if you don't pay. Why not just send them the money? You'd feel much better if you did.'
5 'I think you ought to get in touch with "Safeguard".'
6 'Please, you must help me! I don't know what to do!'
7 'All right, Mr Lock. We'll look into it immediately.'
8 'No, I'm afraid that's not good enough. As I said before, we want to speak to the Sales Manager in person.'
9 'Very well, then – we'll give Mr Lock his deposit back.'
10 'To be honest, after my experience with them, I wouldn't buy anything from Bargain Electrics if I were you.'

6.6 CONVERSATIONS   Free practice

Work in groups.
Tell the others about a conversation you remember in which:
either someone tried to persuade you to do something
or   someone accused you of doing something
or   someone tried to deceive you
or   someone misunderstood you

1 Choose one of the story outlines below and decide:
  a) exactly what happened
  b) how the person was persuaded to change his/her mind
2 Write the story of what happened, reporting any conversation that took
   place.

6.8 MURDER!

Reading

Read the passage below, and see if you can solve the murder.

'An extraordinary case, Holmes,' said Inspector Lestrade, smiling, 'but quite simple, really. We made an arrest immediately.'

'I see,' said Sherlock Holmes, lighting his pipe. 'Tell me about it.'

'Well,' Lestrade began, 'first the people. Old Sir Clarence Forbes married his second wife – the present Lady Forbes – just a year or two ago: very attractive, long dark hair, and young enough to be his daughter. He has a son, too, George, who's 22, and a bit of a disappointment to the old man. Which is why he made this rather strange will.'

Holmes raised his eyebrows. 'Go on.'

'Well, he clearly wants his son to get married and settle down,' continued Lestrade. 'The will says that when he dies half his fortune is to go to his wife, and half to the son – but only if the son is married.'

'And if not?'

'Then it all goes to the wife.' Lestrade paused. 'Well, to cut a long story short, the son is – or was – about to get married. To a local girl called Anna Young. The wedding was to be next month.'

'Was?' asked Sherlock Holmes.

'Yes. This morning Anna Young was found dead – shot through the head – in Lady Forbes' dressing room. The gun was in her hand, and there was a suicide note by the body. It said "Forgive me. I can't live with my guilt any more."'

'And what guilt was that?' Holmes asked.

'I'm coming to that. According to George Forbes, Anna had once had an affair with the family chauffeur – a man called Grimes. And it turns out that Lady Forbes wanted to get all Sir Clarence's fortune for her self. She threatened to tell Sir Clarence about this affair if George didn't cancel the wedding. And there's no doubt that Sir Clarence would have stopped the wedding if he had known.'

'And the chauffeur?'

'Oh, he's out of it. He was out in the car all morning and didn't return till after lunch. Anyway, nowadays he's more interested in Lady Forbes – and she apparently doesn't discourage him. There was a bit of trouble between him and George the other day. They had a quarrel, and Grimes hit George and broke his glasses. Sir Clarence is out of it too – he was out in the car

with Grimes when the murder took place.'

'And why,' asked Holmes, 'do you say it was murder and not suicide?'

'Well for one thing the gun was in the dead girl's right hand, and we know she was left-handed. But the big mistake was the suicide note. We checked the handwriting, and do you know whose writing it was? Lady Forbes'! Of all the stupid mistakes to make.'

'So who have you arrested?'

'Lady Forbes! Who else? She denies everything, of course. She claims that she heard the shot while she was in the bath – next to the dressing room – and that she put a towel round her and rushed out to find Anna on the floor. But she's guilty, all right. She thought her threat to tell Sir Clarence wouldn't work, and decided to stop the wedding properly – by killing Anna Young. She had plenty of time to fake the suicide, too.'

'Hmm,' said Holmes. 'Tell me, Lestrade. Am I right in thinking that Anna Young was dark-haired?'

'Why, yes,' replied Lestrade, in a surprised voice. 'But – how did you know that? That's got nothing to do with . . .'

'I'm afraid, my friend,' said Holmes, 'that you've arrested the wrong person.'

(With apologies to Sir Arthur Conan Doyle)

1 a) Explain the terms of Sir Clarence Forbes' will.
  b) Why did he make his will like this?

2 a) What was Anna Young's secret?
  b Why did she want it to remain a secret?
  c) Why did Lady Forbes not want it to remain a secret?

3 a) What two indications were there that Anna's death had been suicide?
  b) What two reasons did Lestrade have for deciding that her death had in fact been murder?

4 a) According to Lestrade, what motive did Lady Forbes have for murdering Anna?
  b) Can you see a weakness in his reasoning?

5 What alibis did the other three suspects have?

6 Complete the following sentences
  a Lestrade accused Lady Forbes . . .
  b) Lady Forbes denied . . .
  c) Lady Forbes threatened . . .
  d) Lady Forbes claimed . . .

7 Why was Lestrade surprised by Sherlock Holmes' questions about the dark hair? Give two reasons.

Discussion

In groups, try and solve the murder. In your discussion, talk about:
1 the possible motives of George, Sir Clarence and Grimes for the murder
2 George's fight with Grimes
3 the suicide note
4 Sherlock Holmes' question about the colour of Anna's hair

Writing

Write a paragraph explaining who you think murdered Anna Young, how it was done, and why.

(The murderer's confession can be found on p. 165.)

Unit 6 Summary of language

In this unit, you have learnt how to:
– report what you and other people said
– report what you and other people thought

KEY POINTS

1 *Reported speech structures*
  She told me she **was** expecting a baby.
  He said he **hadn't** been there before.
  But you told me I **would** enjoy it!
  He said that he **was going to** meet a friend.

2 *'Reported thought' structures*
  I thought he **was** a bachelor.
  I didn't realise they**'d** bought a dog.

3 *Reporting verbs: statements*
  He **claimed** (**that**) he had climbed Everest.
  I **warned** him (**that**) he would catch malaria.
  She **accused** him **of** ly**ing** to her.
  He **insisted** (**that**) he had met her.

4 *Reporting verbs: influencing and taking action*
  He **threatened to** call the police.
  He **begged** her **to** marry him.
  I **suggested** (**that**) she **should** contact the Embassy.
  He **insisted on** carry**ing** my suitcase.

Activities

SHORTLIST

Four package-tour companies have advertised for a local tourist guide to take groups of British tourists to see places of interest. From the many applications, each company has selected a shortlist of four applicants, and has sent out an interview board from Britain to make the final selection. The interview board will choose a tourist guide on the basis of:
1 knowledge of local tourist spots
2 previous experience as a tourist guide
3 ability to organise, and to deal with problems
4 suitable personality

Students A, B, C and D: You are the four applicants who are going to be interviewed. Think of what you will say in your interview.

Groups 1, 2, 3 and 4: You are the interview boards from the four companies. Think of the questions you will ask the four applicants in your interviews.

In turn, the four applicants are interviewed by the four boards.

After the interviews:
1 each board says which applicant it has chosen, and why
2 each applicant says which tourist company he/she would prefer to work for, and why

COMPOSITION

Write 120–180 words on one of these topics:
1 Tourists
2 You work as a tourist guide for one of the companies above. Say what the job is like.
3 Explain which of the four applicants is most suitable for the job of tourist guide.

SITUATIONS

1 Your boy/girlfriend didn't turn up for a date last night, and phoned this morning to explain. Tell someone what he/she said.

2 Someone asks you how long the Post Office takes to deliver a letter. What do you reply?

3 A friend asks you about a programme you saw/heard on TV/the radio last week. Tell him/her what you thought of it.

4 In a job interview you are asked what sort of people you get on with. What do you say?

5 You had an argument with someone the other day about parking your car. Tell a friend what happened.

6 You meet a friend you haven't seen for three months. Bring him/her up to date about yourself.

7 You arrive late at a meeting, after being delayed by traffic. Apologise and explain why you are late.

Unit 7 Deductions and explanations

7.1 MUST, MIGHT, MAY & CAN'T   Presentation 🔊

You will hear three short dialogues, in which people make deductions.

Dialogue 1

What does the woman say about:

1 George's pay? ....

2 George's car? ....

What does the man say about:

3 George's pay? ....

4 George's suit? ....

Dialogue 2

What does the woman say about:

1 a snack? ....

2 a curry? ....

3 a restaurant? ....

What does the man say about:

4 how far Hilda's gone? ....

Dialogue 3

What does the man say about:

1 bed? ....

2 start/smoking again? ....

What does the woman say about:

3 the pipe? ....

4 breathing? ....

⋙→

Change the sentences below, using **must**, **can't** and **might/may**.

1 I'm sure he's working.
2 Perhaps he's going to ask me.
3 I'm sure he's not French.
4 I'm sure they stole the money.
5 Perhaps he was listening.
6 I'm sure she wasn't at work.
7 Perhaps he went home.

8 Perhaps she's not coming.
9 I'm sure they weren't camping.
10 Perhaps they haven't finished.
11 Perhaps he was tired.
12 I'm sure she was feeling ill.
13 I'm sure the snow's melted.
14 I'm sure they haven't been waiting long.

7.2   WORKING IT OUT   Practice

Answer the questions in Column A using **must** or **can't**, giving a reason from Column B.

Example   He can't have gone abroad because he hasn't got a passport.

A	B
Did he go abroad?	The line's engaged.
Has he been working hard?	He had it done only a month ago.
Is he redecorating his house?	It only cost him £15.
Is he an Indian?	He was only promoted last week.
Has the meat gone off?	He got a lot of post this morning.
Is he talking on the phone?	He hasn't got a passport.
Is the table an antique?	It smells terrible.
Is it his birthday?	He looks exhausted.
Has he been made redundant?	He's got fair hair.

Work in pairs. Continue the sentences below with a deduction.

Example   A: Her bedroom light's on ...
            B: ... so she can't be asleep.
                ... so she can't have gone out.
                ... so she must be reading in bed.
                ... so she must have gone to bed.

1 He's got a lovely suntan ...
2 She's driving a Mercedes ...
3 They didn't come to the party ...
4 He isn't wearing a uniform ...
5 She speaks excellent French ...
6 I can hear music next door ...

Look at the pictures below, and answer the questions, giving reasons for your deductions.

Picture 1

1 Do you think they are:
   a) friends?
   b) strangers?
   c) father and daughter?

2 Are they:
   a) in the street?
   b) in a park?
   c) in the garden?

3 Which is true?
   a) He's just caught sight of her.
   b) They've just had an argument.
   c) They're having a walk together.

Picture 2

1 Do you think the three people are:
   a) three friends?
   b) a couple and a waiter?
   c) a couple and a stranger?

2 Is the man on the right:
   a) sitting down?
   b) getting up to greet them?
   c) getting up to leave?

3 Is the woman:
   a) taking off her coat?
   b) putting on her coat?

Picture 3

1 Do you think he is:
   a) at home?
   b) at a friend's house?
   c) at a hotel?

2 When the phone rang, do you think he was:
   a) getting ready for bed?
   b) asleep?
   c) getting up?

3 Is he:
   a) picking up the phone?
   b) putting down the phone?

7.4 DEDUCTIONS AND REASONS: 'IF'

Presentation

Look at the paragraphs below, and answer the questions using 'If . . .'

1 'I wonder what those lights are up there. They can't be from a hill-top
restaurant, or anything like that, because they're moving. And they can't be
car lights because they're all different colours. Perhaps it's an aeroplane – no,
it can't be that, either – there's no engine noise, and anyway they're not
flashing on and off . . .'

How do we know that the lights can't be:
a) a hill-top restaurant?
b) a car?
c) an aeroplane?

2 'He claims that he's a doctor, that he's lived in Cyprus most of his life, and
that he's never been to America, but he's lying. When I mentioned "hepatitis"
the other day, he thought it was a kind of insect. He's got a US stamp in his
passport, and when we went to a Greek restaurant last night, he couldn't
understand a word the waiter said . . .'

How do we know the man:
a) can't be a doctor?
b) can't have lived in Cyprus most of his life?
c) must have been to America?

Practice

Example A: I'm sure she's going to leave me.
   B: Nonsense. If she was going to leave you, she wouldn't have agreed
      to go on holiday with you.
   C: And what's more, she wouldn't have invited you to meet her
      parents.
   D: And if she was going to leave you, she wouldn't be redecorating
      your kitchen for you, would she?

Work in groups. Have similar conversations, beginning with the remarks
below.
1 I'm sure he/she's in love with me.
2 I'm sure he didn't steal the money.
3 I think they're going to declare war.
4 I wonder if that fish was off.
5 She says she's a socialist.
6 I'm sure I'm going to get the sack.
7 I think I've got gangrene in my leg.

Work in groups. Discuss one of the three statements below. What arguments might be used for or against them? What is your own opinion, and why?

1 There is intelligent life on other planets.
2 UFOs are the product of people's imaginations.
3 Some ancient monuments (e.g. the Pyramids) were built by beings from outer space.

Report your conclusions to the rest of the class.

7.6   EXPLANATIONS

Practice

You will hear someone talking about prison. Listen to the tape and answer the questions.
1 What fact is the speaker attempting to explain?
2 What do a lot of people think this indicates?
3 What two alternative explanations does he give?
4 To what extent do you agree with him? Can you think of any other explanations?

Work in groups. Discuss the facts below. What might they **indicate/suggest/mean**?
1 Football hooliganism is becoming an increasingly serious problem in Britain.
2 Since divorce became easier to obtain in Britain, the divorce rate has gone up dramatically.
3 In recent years, there has been a growing interest in magic and the occult in Europe and America.
4 My grandfather smoked all his life, and lived till he was 90.

⫸→

Writing

Write a paragraph about one of the topics you discussed. Examine the possible explanations, and come to a conclusion.

7.7 PERSONALITY QUIZ   Free practice

1 Mark your own answers in the personality quiz below.
2 Look at your partner's answers, and tell him/her what each one indicates about his/her personality.
3 Tell him/her in general how good a party-goer you think he/she would be.

Are you the perfect party-goer?

1. How do you feel about strangers?
    Do you find them
    (a) fascinating?
    (b) rather frightening?
    (c) somewhere in between?

2. Which kind of parties do you prefer?
    (a) small, quiet parties?
    (b) big, noisy parties?
    (c) parties with dancing and games?
    (d) no parties at all?

3. You find yourself standing with a complete stranger at a party. Would you
    (a) talk about yourself?
    (b) talk about the weather?
    (c) try to get him/her to talk about him/herself?

4. Someone invites you to a fancy dress party at very short notice. Would you
    (a) go without fancy dress?
    (b) not go?
    (c) improvise a quick costume out of anything you could find?

5. Some friends have invited you to a dinner party at very short notice. You know they've been planning the party for quite a long time, and you suspect that they've only invited you because someone else has dropped out. Would you
   (a) accept with pleasure?
   (b) refuse indignantly?
   (c) accept, but let them know they've hurt your feelings?

6. You're not sure whether you're expected to take anything to a party. Would you
   (a) ring up and ask?
   (b) not take anything?
   (c) take a bottle anyway?

7. At the party, would you
   (a) tend to drink too much?
   (b) stick to soft drinks?
   (c) drink just enough to let yourself go?

8. Someone spends a lot of time dancing with your partner. Would you
   (a) sit down and feel miserable?
   (b) not mind at all?
   (c) show your partner you're having a great time dancing with other people?
   (d) try and take your partner away from him/her?

9. There are some games at the party. Would you
   (a) join in enthusiastically?
   (b) sit at the side looking superior?
   (c) join in, but think it's rather childish?

10. It's late, and it's clear that the host and hostess want to go to bed. Would you
    (a) say goodnight and leave?
    (b) carry on enjoying yourself?
    (c) ask if you can help clear up before you go?

Reading

On 2 April 1973, Dr R. S. Griffiths, of Manchester University, was walking home when a solid object crashed into the street only three metres away from him, smashing into
5 several pieces. It was a solid block of ice, and, as a scientist, Dr Griffiths immediately realised its significance. He picked up the largest piece and ran home to put it in his deep-freeze; as a result, it became the best-studied example of a
10 phenomenon so far unexplained by science.

Dr Griffiths' ice-block wasn't particularly big – 612 grams – but there are countless recorded examples much larger than that, all of them much larger than the heaviest
15 hailstones, which rarely weigh more than 200 grams. These ice-blocks have smashed through the roofs of houses, dented the metal of cars, and even killed sheep.

Griffiths demonstrated scientifically that his
20 block could not have been a large hailstone. Nor could it have dropped from a passing aircraft, as the flight records of the only two aeroplanes in the area showed.

Nine seconds before Griffiths' block fell,
25 there had been a stroke of lightning. Might these large ice-blocks, then, be produced by lightning? Or could they come from space? Scientists at the Drexel Institute in the USA concluded that 'the large chunks of ice which
30 have fallen could not have been meteorological in origin', while scientists at Colorado University said that though there could be ice out in space, such blocks of ice probably couldn't survive the intense heat when entering
35 our atmosphere.

The usual explanation that ice-blocks 'must have fallen from aeroplanes' applies only in a few cases: all modern planes have automatic de-icing equipment, and in any case there are
40 many reports of huge blocks of ice from pre-aircraft days.

Another interesting example of an ice-fall happened in Timberville, Virginia on 7 March

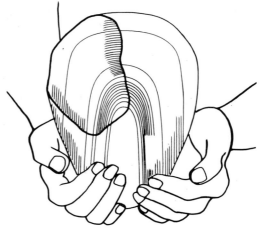

Size of ice-block recovered from road in Manchester after falling from sky, 2 April 1973.
(Bold outline describes shape of fragment preserved in freezer.)

1976. At about 8.45, three people were watching television when a loud crash shook 45 their house and a block of ice the size of a basketball smashed through the roof and a ceiling and ended up in the living room. And as if someone up there was giving a repeat performance, 20 seconds later another ice- 50 block crashed to the ground less than 50 metres away.

These falls were explained, after an official investigation, as being drinking water that had leaked from a plane, frozen on the fuselage, 55 and broken off in 5–6 kilo pieces. In fact, it was a clear night, there were no planes in the sky, and the source of the blocks must, logically, have remained still in the sky for 20 seconds. Despite all such 'explanations', the 60 problem of where such large blocks of ice can come from remains absolutely unsolved.

(Adapted from *The World Atlas of Mysteries*)

1 'a phenomenon so far unexplained by science' (line 10). What phenomenon is the writer referring to?

2 What *two* conclusions did Dr Griffiths come to about the ice-block he had found?

3 The writer mentions three general 'explanations' for falling ice-blocks.
  a) What are they?
  b) Why does he reject them?

4 a) What was the official explanation for the Timberville ice-blocks?
  b) In rejecting this explanation, why does the writer mention the following facts?
    i) The night was clear.
    ii) There was a 20-second gap between the two ice-falls.

5 According to the writer, there have been 'countless recorded examples' of falling ice-blocks. Why do you think he chose to describe:
  a) the one in Manchester?
  b) the one in Timberville?

6 a) Do you find the writer's evidence and conclusions convincing?
  b) What explanation would *you* give for the events he describes?

Writing

Write 100–150 words about ice-falls. Without mentioning any particular examples, say:
1 what they are
2 what explanations have been put forward
3 why these are unsatisfactory
4 what you think

Unit 7 Summary of language

In this unit, you have learnt how to:
- make deductions
- give reasons for deductions
- explain the significance of situations and events

KEY POINTS

1 *Modals and infinitives*
He **must** earn a lot.
They **might** not **be** coming to visit us.
He **must have** met her before.
They **can't have been** living there long.

2 *Conditional structures*
If he **didn't** earn a lot, he **wouldn't** wear such expensive clothes.
If they **were coming** to visit us, they **would have** telephoned.
If he **hadn't met** her, he **wouldn't** know her name.

3 *'Significance' structures*
The fact that he's got the sack **doesn't necessarily mean that** he was bad at his job – it **may have been because** the manager didn't like him.
Winters are getting colder – this **may indicate that** there's another ice-age coming.

Activities

OUT AND ABOUT

You work for a local newspaper which is running a series of articles called 'Out and About'. For each article, you ask people in the street about one particular public place or service in the town (e.g. a sports centre, a restaurant, a club): what is their experience of it, and what do they think of it?

Work in pairs.
1 Choose a subject for your article. Think of some questions you might ask.
2 Interview as many people as you can, taking brief notes. Other people will interview you too. Answer their questions.
3 Report back to the class, summarising what you have found out about people's attitudes.

COMPOSITION

Using the notes you made, write an article (120–180 words) for the series 'Out and About'.
Include the following:
− a brief description of the place or service you chose
− a general summary of what people thought of it
− any particular comments you heard which are of special interest

Unit 8   Advantages and disadvantages

8.1   GOOD AND BAD EFFECTS

Presentation

You will hear a story about the island of Tango, a small island in the South
Pacific. Listen to the tape and answer the questions.

1 What effect did the drug have on people's minds?
2 What effect did it have on the country's economy, and why?
3 What did the Government do, and why weren't they successful?
4 What did the Government do in the end, and why was this a better solution?

Listen to the tape again. Choosing verbs from the list, write sentences which
have the same meaning as those below. Begin with the words given.

allow	stop	make it easier
enable	prevent	make it more difficult
encourage	discourage	
force	save	

1 When they took the drug, it was more difficult for them to think rationally.
   The drug . . .
2 When they took the drug, they didn't worry about the future.
   The drug . . .
3 When they took the drug, they were able to forget all their problems.
   The drug . . .
4 When they took the drug, they could relax and enjoy themselves more easily.
   The drug . . .
5 Although there was a shortage of food, people still wanted to take the drug.
   Even the food shortage didn't . . .
6 Because of the economic crisis, the Government had to take some decisive
   action.
   The economic crisis . . .
7 After the new law was introduced, people still took the drug.
   The new law didn't . . .
8 After the new law was introduced, people wanted to take the drug even
   more.
   The new law . . .
9 When the drug was exported, the islanders didn't have to work more than
   one day a week.
   Exporting the drug . . .
10 When the drug was exported, they were able to sit in the sun all day long.
   This . . .

Practice

Student A: You are a spokesman for the Government of Tango.
Student B: You are a reporter. Interview Student A. You want to know:
    1 the advantages and disadvantages of allowing people to take the drug
    2 the disadvantages of making the drug illegal
    3 the advantages and disadvantages of Tango's present policy

8.2 PROS AND CONS   Practice

Example: package holidays
    A: Package holidays enable people to travel abroad cheaply.
    B: Ah yes, but they discourage people from being adventurous, because everything is organised for them.
    C: But on the other hand, they make it easier for single people to make friends on holiday.
    D: Yes, but they force you to spend your holiday with people you may not like.
    A: ...

Work in groups. In the same way, talk about the advantages and disadvantages of the following. Use the verbs from 8.1.

1 credit cards
2 having a beard
3 television
4 having a telephone
5 being rich and famous
6 having a freezer
7 practising English in groups

8.3 ADVANTAGES AND DISADVANTAGES

Presentation

Read the passage below, and answer the questions.

Most people are much more frightened of being unemployed than they need to be. Being unemployed certainly has disadvantages, but there are good things about it too. One advantage of not having a job is that you don't have to get up early and go to work in the rush hour. You can stay in bed as long as you like, and there's plenty of time to read the newspaper and have a leisurely breakfast. But the best thing of all is that you're your own boss – there's no one to tell you what to do and when to do it.

One drawback of being unemployed is, of course, that you haven't got much money coming in – having a job at least enables you to save a bit of money to go on holiday. On the other hand, when you're unemployed you don't need to go on holiday, because you're on holiday already. In fact the main trouble with being unemployed is that you have to spend so much of your time looking for a job.

1   What does the writer consider to be (a) the main advantage (b) the main disadvantage of being unemployed?
2   To what extent do you agree with him? What do you consider the main advantages and disadvantages to be?

Use the expressions below:
advantage   disadvantage   trouble
good thing   bad thing   drawback

Free practice

Work in groups. Discuss whether you think it is preferable to live in your own country or abroad. What are the advantages and disadvantages of each?

Writing

Write a paragraph based on your discussion. Say which you think is preferable, and why.

8.4 COURSES OF ACTION   Presentation and practice

1 Which of the expressions used by the four people above means:

   a) it's a good thing to do
   b) it's a bad thing to do
   c) it won't do any good
   d) it won't do any harm

2 Change the suggestions below, using **ought to**, **ought not to**, **might as well** or **there's no point in**.

   Example: Let's not take the lift – he only lives on the first floor.
        There's no point in taking the lift.

   1 Don't take your children to see that film – it'll frighten them.
   2 Let's not sell it – it's not worth anything anyway.
   3 Why don't we give it away – it's not worth anything anyway.
   4 Don't ask him – he doesn't speak English.
   5 Why don't you take a pullover – you've got plenty of room in your case.
   6 Why don't you take a pullover – it might turn cold.
   7 Let's not talk about it now – the children are listening.
   8 Let's not argue about it – that won't solve the problem.

8.5 ADVISING ON A CHOICE   Practice

Example A: Shall we go by bus?

   B: No, | **there's no point in** | waiting for the bus – it's only a short distance.
           | **it's not worth** |

   C: Yes, we **might as well** walk.

Work in threes. Have similar conversations, beginning with the remarks below.
1 Do you think I should keep all these old clothes?
2 What shall we do with the money? Invest it?
3 Should I send this letter first class?
4 Let's get a bigger washing machine.
5 Maybe we ought to keep some of this ice cream for Mary.
6 Do you think we should go to school today?
7 I think I'll make a bookcase.

Work in groups of three. You are students A, B and C.
Read through your own section only, and then play the game, starting with
Student A.
Examples (Don't open the window)

        A: You'd better not open the window . . .

B or C: You'll get soaked.

        A: It's no use opening the window . . .

B or C: It's even hotter outside.

Student A
Read out sentences 1–3 twice:
a) with **You'd better not**
b) with **There's no point in . . .ing** or **It's no use . . .ing**
Students B and C will complete them.

1 Don't pick up your gun:
2 Don't run away:
3 Don't lock the door:

Choose one of these sentences to complete what B and C read out, so that your continuation makes sense.

. . . they might poison you.
. . . he doesn't know what he's done.
. . . lots of people would like to have your job.
. . . you'll probably offend her.
. . . he's terribly stingy.
. . . he won't be back until tomorrow.
. . . he's totally incorruptible.
. . . his mother will complain.
. . . you'll be late for the theatre.
. . . he might report you to the police.
. . . she hasn't even told her best friends.
. . . they won't have any effect.

Student B
Read out sentences 1–3 twice:
a) with **You'd better not**
b) with **There's no point in . . .ing** or **It's no use . . .ing**
Students A and C will complete them.

1 Don't wait for Mr Jenkins:
2 Don't try to bribe him:
3 Don't ask him for a rise in salary:

Choose one of these sentences to complete what A and C read out, so that your continuation makes sense.

. . . you'll get your fingerprints on it.
. . . his mother will complain.
. . . you'll probably offend her.
. . . people will think you're guilty.
. . . they won't have any effect.
. . . it's not loaded.
. . . they've got skeleton keys.
. . . they might poison you.
. . . he doesn't know what he's done.
. . . they'll find you in no time.
. . . John may not have a key.
. . . she hasn't even told her best friends.

Student C
Read out sentences 1–3 twice:
a) with **You'd better not**
b) with **There's no point in . . .ing** or **It's no use . . .ing**
Students A and B will complete them.

1 Don't take those pills:
2 Don't punish him:
3 Don't ask her how old she is:

Choose one of these sentences to complete what A and B read out, so that your continuation makes sense.

. . . lots of people would like to have your job.
. . . he's totally incorruptible.
. . . John may not have a key.
. . . people will think you're guilty.
. . . you'll be late for the theatre.
. . . you'll get your fingerprints on it.
. . . he might report you to the police.
. . . it's not loaded.
. . . he's terribly stingy.
. . . they've got skeleton keys.
. . . they'll find you in no time.
. . . he won't be back until tomorrow.

8.7   WHAT WOULD HAPPEN?

Presentation and practice

Sam is 17, and is about to leave school. He's not sure what he wants to do, but he's vaguely interested in business . . .

One possibility would be for him to go on to a college of further education. If he did that, he would have more qualifications, and that would enable him to get a better job at the end of it. One problem would be that he wouldn't earn any money while he was there, but he could always work in the evenings and get holiday jobs.

In the same way, talk about what you think would happen (and what the advantages and disadvantages would be) if Sam:
1 did a variety of temporary jobs for a few months
2 travelled abroad for a year
3 joined a firm straight away

Free practice

Work in groups. Tell the others about a difficult choice you have to make in your own life.
Discuss the various possibilities open to you, and the advantages and disadvantages of each. Get them to help you decide what to do.

Use this list of topics to help you:
family life   relationships
career   money

Writing

Choose one of the problems you discussed. Write a letter to the person
concerned and:
- suggest possible courses of action
- mention the advantages and disadvantages of each
- advise him/her what to (and not to) do

8.8 DISHWASHERS

Reading

Over the last fifty years housework has been
made considerably easier by the invention of
an increasing number of labour-saving devices
and appliances, mostly electrical, which have
5 drastically cut down the amount of time and
effort previously needed to do the everyday
household chores. For many years now there
have been vacuum cleaners, electric irons,
washing machines and floor-polishers; now
10 we have electric potato-peelers and even
electric carving knives. We can buy cookers
that will switch themselves on and produce a
meal that is ready to eat the minute we get
back home. If we have one of those electric
15 pop-up toasters, we can make toast at the
breakfast table itself. Mashed potatoes can be
quickly and effortlessly made with a mixer,
which usually has a variety of attachments
that enable you to make all sorts of other more
20 exotic things like fresh orange juice or real
mayonnaise. And a tumble-drier can save you
from the frustration of hanging out the
washing only to have to bring it in again ten
minutes later when menacing storm-clouds
25 loom over.

Probably the most important piece of
electrical equipment to become widely used in
the last twenty years is the dishwasher.
Washing up by hand is not only a time-
30 consuming task (it can take longer than eating
the meal itself), but also an extremely boring
one, particularly when you are on your own,
and it also ruins your hands. Dishwashers
come in a range of different sizes and models
35 to suit your purse, the size of your family, and
the layout of your kitchen. They can be stood
on the floor or on a worktop, or they can be
mounted on a wall. And their capacity ranges
from six to twelve place-settings. If you buy
one, it is worth having it plumbed into the   40
mains water supply to save you having to
connect rubber pipes to your taps each time
you use it. All you have to do is load the dirty
dishes, glasses and cutlery into the racks inside
the machine, pour in some special detergent   45
powder, close the door and switch it on; it
does the rest by itself while you get on and do
more interesting things. Of course, most
dishwashers can't accommodate large
saucepans and frying pans, and you do have to 50
scrape all scraps of solid food from the dishes
before you put them in to avoid blocking the
filters, but the machine will wash almost
everything else and get rid of even the most
stubborn egg and lipstick stains. When the   55
washing cycle is over, the machine dries the
plates and glasses with its own heat, and
indeed they can be left inside until they are
needed for the next meal.

If you buy a medium-sized dishwasher, you   60
probably won't need to wash up more than
once a day. The drawback of this, of course, is
that you have to have enough dishes, cutlery,
etc to last three or four meals. So it can happen
that people who buy a dishwasher have to buy   65
new china and glasses, either because they
haven't got enough or because the ones they've
got don't fit the machine. This extra expense
may not only be necessary, but also desirable,
for one has to remember that dishwashers can   70
be quite noisy. This means that many people
prefer only to use their machine once a day,
preferably last thing at night, when you can
just shut the kitchen door on it and go to bed.

1 In one sentence each, explain what the writer tells us in:
   a) the first paragraph   b) the second paragraph   c) the third paragraph

80

2 Do you think the writer is generally in favour of labour-saving devices? How can you tell?

3 Explain in your own words the advantages of:
   a) automatic cookers   c) mashing potatoes with a mixer
   b) electric pop-up toasters   d) tumble-driers.
   What disadvantages (if any) do you think there might be?

4 Explain the meaning of:
   a) 'everyday household chores' (lines 6–7)
   b) 'menacing storm-clouds loom over' (lines 24–5)
   c) 'to suit your purse' (line 35)
   Why does the writer call fresh orange juice and real mayonnaise 'exotic' (line 20)?

5 Which of these claims about dishwashers are true, and which are false?
   a) They can be hung on the wall.   d) They get rid of stains.
   b) They have a special place for large   e) They dry dishes by blowing hot air through
      saucepans and frying pans.   them.
   c) They get rid of scraps of solid food.   f) They switch themselves off.

6 Why might you want to buy more china and cutlery when you get a dishwasher? Give two reasons.

Writing

1 In the columns below, list in note form the advantages and disadvantages of dishwashers mentioned in the passage.

Advantages	Disadvantages

2 Expand your notes into a paragraph of 100–120 words, summarising the main advantages and disadvantages of having a dishwasher.

Unit 8 Summary of language

In this unit, you have learnt how to:
– talk about advantages and disadvantages
– talk about good and bad effects
– give advice and make suggestions
– discuss possible courses of action and their consequences

KEY POINTS

1 *'Effect' verbs*
Advertisements **encourage** people **to** spend more money.
Having a degree **enables** you **to** get a better job.
The new law **prevented** people **from** travel**ling** freely.
Having a washing machine **saves** you (from) hav**ing** to do the washing by hand.

2 *'Advantage/disadvantage' structures*
One **advantage of** be**ing** a student **is that** you can get cheap train tickets.
The trouble with liv**ing** in a flat **is that** you don't have a garden.
The main **drawback of** motorbikes **is that** they're so noisy.

3 *Advice and suggestions*
There's no point in tak**ing** a taxi – it isn't far.
It's not worth book**ing** a seat in advance – it's never full.
It's no use ask**ing** him – he doesn't know.
We **might as well** go to bed – he won't come now.

4 *Conditional structures*
If you **went** to university you **could** get a degree, and that **would** enable you to get a better job. The only problem **would** be that you**'d** have to leave home.

82

Activities

ıck is designed
ıbility and
ɔnomy.
.6 tons.
ınd a range
s. With a
ansmissions.
ıns profit,

Lord Cramford: slum landlord?

Lord Cramford, the controversial campaigner for prison reform and millionaire property owner, has become the centre of another scandal, this time over the thirty or so flats and houses in London which he lets out to tenants.

All of these properties, according to Mrs Angela Dickenson of the Tenants' Association, are slums.

Rats

A report published today says they are 'unfit for human habitation', and goes on to claim:

- The rents are too high.
- They're damp and many of the roofs leak.
- They're infested with rats.
- Only 30% of the flats have proper bathrooms.
- They all need extensive repairs and redecoration.

Criminals

'Lord Cramford seems to me more concerned for the welfare of criminals' commented Mrs Dickenson, 'than of his tenants.

'Personally, I would be surprised if any prisoners in this country were living in such appalling conditions as Lord Cramford's tenants.

'These buildings are slums.'

Malicious

Lord Cramford today reacted angrily to these charges: 'They're malicious nonsense', he claimed.

'I have had all my properties extensively modernised. But the area is plagued with vandals, who are continually causing damage, and the police and the tenants do nothing to stop them.

'I cannot do everything myself—the tenants must play their part too.

'As for the rents, they are fixed by the Rent Office, not by me!'

⋙→

Work in three groups.

Group A: You are a reporter, and you are going to conduct a television
interview with Lord Cramford and Mrs Dickenson. You want to find
out what truth there is in the allegations, and what action both of
them intend to take. Think what questions you will ask.

Group B: You are Mrs Dickenson. You are going to be interviewed on
television about the Tenants' Association's allegations, and about
what action you intend to take.
Think what you will say.

Group C: You are Lord Cramford. You are going to be interviewed on
television about the Tenants' Association's allegations, and about
what action you intend to take.
Think what you will say.

Now form new groups of three (one A, one B and one C) and conduct the
interview.

COMPOSITION

Write a short newspaper report (120–180 words) of your discussion.

Unit 9 Clarifying

9.1 INFORMATION QUESTIONS   Presentation and practice

When we get to the crossroads, **which way do we go?**

Change the questions below to information questions, as in the example.

1 Are we having *tomato/chicken/mushroom* soup today?
2 Was it *raining/foggy/cold* when you were in London?
3 Are you planning to use *your father's car/Tony's car/my car*?
4 Are you going to *boil/fry/scramble* those eggs?
5 Is it *500 miles/1000 miles/a long way* to London from here?
6 Would you like to do *manual/office/outdoor* work?
7 Are there *four/five/six* of you?
8 I hear he's hurt his leg. Has he *broken/bruised/cut* it?
9 Are you Margaret's *cousin/brother/nephew*?
10 Is the cinema *opposite/next to/round the corner from* the station?
11 Have you *given away/sold/burnt* my old football boots?
12 Did you use *half-inch/one-inch/three-quarter-inch* screws?

Look at the sets of words below, and (a) decide what each set has in common (b) ask an information question about it.

1 arson/blackmail/assault
2 stew/grill/roast
3 major/sergeant/corporal
4 primary/grammar/comprehensive
5 Ford/Volkswagen/Citroën
6 rubber/leather/plastic
7 A4/foolscap/quarto
8 crimson/scarlet/maroon
9 rare/medium/well done
10 A/B/C

Example A: Don't disturb me – I'm thinking.

B: | Really? | |
    | Oh, are you? | What are you thinking about?

A: I'm wondering what to say to my wife when I get home.

B: Why, have you had a row with her?

Work in pairs. Have short conversations, as in the example. Begin with the sentences below.

1 My sister got engaged last week.
2 He died suddenly at the age of 35.
3 I'm going to wrap those Christmas presents.
4 I'm sure John's in love.
5 Can I borrow your penknife for a moment?

6 James says he wants to talk to you.
7 They've just sold their flat.
8 I spent the evening playing chess last night.
9 They're going to convert their attic.

9.3   INDIRECT QUESTIONS

Presentation

Examples What are golf balls made of?
Do you know **what** golf balls **are made of**?

Have the election results been announced yet?

Do you know | **if** | |
             | **whether** | the election results **have been announced** yet?

Rewrite the following questions as indirect questions, as in the examples. Begin with the words given.

1 What time did you wake up this morning?
   Can you remember . . . ?
2 How much do colour TVs cost these days?
   Have you any idea . . . ?
3 What time does the film start?
   I wonder . . .
4 Was he alone?
   Did you notice . . . ?

5 When are they getting married?
   I'm longing to know . . .
6 Did I lock the front door?
   Do you remember . . . ?
7 Has the train left?
   Have you found out . . . ?
8 What colour curtains did they buy?
   Do you know . . . ?

Practice

Work in groups. Use the expressions above to ask the others questions about:
1 their childhood
2 what's going on in the world
3 other people in the class

A policeman is questioning a witness about an incident he saw in the street.
Look at the witness's answers, and decide what questions he is being asked.

. . . He was about ten metres from the telephone box, talking . . .

. . . To a woman – she was in her late twenties, and wearing a scarf and a long
   black coat . . .

. . . Leather, I think, with a wide belt. She had a dog with her, on a lead . . .

. . . I'm not sure. It could have been some kind of terrier. Anyway, they kept
   looking at a group of men who were standing on the other side of the street . . .

. . . Oh, at least six or seven, I'd say . . .

. . . Well, a blue car came up and stopped suddenly by the telephone box . . .

. . . It was one of those Japanese cars – it might have been a Datsun . . .

. . . A greeny blue – almost turquoise. And that's when the trouble started . . .

Work in pairs. This is a memory test.
Student A: Look at the picture for about 30 seconds. Then, without looking,
            answer Student B's questions about what you saw.
Student B: Ask Student A about the picture *in as much detail as you can.*

Some friends went on a 'Round Europe' tour recently. In one city they went to the opera, but they can't quite remember which one it was . . .

In the same way, ask three different questions for each of the situations below:

1 You think Andrew left the country on *Saturday*, but you're not sure.
2 You think your friend was dancing with *Mary*, but you're not sure.
3 You think the *Smiths* gave you a Monopoly set for Christmas, but you're not sure.
4 You think there were floods in *Iran* last year, but you're not sure.
5 You think you ordered a *vodka*, but you're not sure.
6 You think *Mozart* wrote the 'Pastoral' Symphony, but you're not sure.
7 You think the 1980 Olympics were held in *Montreal*, but you're not sure.

Work in pairs. Have conversations as in the example, beginning with the questions you have just asked.

A: | Milan was the place where | we went to the opera, wasn't it?
   | It was in Milan that |
B: No, it wasn't – it was in Budapest that we went to the opera.
A: Yes, of course – Milan was the place where we went to the ballet.

9.6 YOU'VE GOT IT ALL WRONG   Practice

You will hear a short conversation between four people, in which the first speaker gets everything wrong. Listen to the tape and answer the questions.
1 What does the first speaker think happened?
2 What three things has he got wrong?
3 What really happened?

Work in groups. Have similar conversations, based on the sentences below. The words in italic show what is incorrect.

1 *Salma* lost her *handbag* at a party at the *French* Embassy.
2 The *postmen* are going on strike *all over* England *tomorrow*.
3 Richard *broke* his *ankle* while he was playing *tennis*.
4 Jane was given a *gold ring* by an *American film star*.
5 His *brother* has *scrambled* eggs for *lunch* every day.

Continue with some sentences of your own.

9.7   REPORTED QUESTIONS

Presentation

'The first man was quite friendly. He wanted to know whether I'd visited Britain before, and how much money I had with me. He asked me how long I was going to stay, and where I could be found if they wanted to get in touch with me. Then another man came in and started asking me the most extraordinary questions: whether I belonged to any terrorist organisations, whether I'd ever taken drugs, what my political views were, why I was coming to Britain in January ... And then, when I asked him what was wrong with coming to Britain in January, he just smiled and gave me back my passport, and let me through ...'

What were the actual questions asked by:
1 the first man?
2 the second man?
3 the speaker himself?

Practice

Here are some questions that the speaker was asked on three other occasions. Report them.

Did you have a good journey?
Are you hungry?
Did you have a meal on the plane?
Did you have any trouble at customs?

How are you feeling?
Have you been vaccinated against cholera?
How much do you smoke?
Do you do any exercise?
Have you been sleeping badly?

Have you worked in a restaurant before?
How far away do you live?
Are you willing to work in the evenings?
When can you start?

9.8   UNDER FIRE

Free practice

Work in groups. Tell the others about an occasion (real or imaginary) when:
either   you were questioned by the police
or   you had an oral examination
or   you had a job interview
or   you were interviewed by the Press

Writing

Write a paragraph describing *either* the story you told *or* one of the stories you heard.

9.9   JOB INTERVIEW

Listening

You will hear a woman talking about a job interview she had. Listen to the tape, and answer the questions.

1 a) What job was the woman interviewed for, and who by?
   b) How successful was she?

2 The interview was very unusual in three different ways. What were they?

3 Write down three things the interviewer wanted to know at the beginning of the interview.

4 a) What had the woman done the year before?
   b) Where in particular had she been and what had she done there?
   c) In what way would this experience be relevant to her new job?

5 Make a list of all the different energy sources the woman mentions.

6 Why, according to the woman, was the interviewer impressed?

7 a) What personal questions did the interviewer ask?
   b) Two possible reasons are suggested for these questions. What are they?

8 What is the woman going to do next week?

Free practice

1 Pair A: From the information on the tape, try to reconstruct what the interviewer actually said during the interview.
   Pair B: From the information on the tape, try to reconstruct what the woman actually said during the interview.

2 Form new pairs. One of you is the interviewer, the other is the woman. Improvise the interview.

Unit 9 Summary of language

In this unit, you have learnt how to:
- ask for precise information
- check on information
- correct people
- report questions people asked

KEY POINTS

1 *Information questions*
 What flavour ice cream do you want?
 Which way did he go?
 How would you like your fish cooked?
 Who is she going out **with**?
 What did he talk to you **about**?

2 *Indirect questions*
 I wonder why he **went** home early.
 Do you know how much that hi-fi **costs**?
 Can you remember where you **left** the keys?

3 *'Tag' questions and 'identifying' structures*
 We arrived on Sunday, **didn't we**?
 Sunday **was the day** (**when**) we arrived, **wasn't it**?
 It was on Sunday **that** we arrived, **wasn't it**?
 It wasn't on Sunday **that** we arrived – **it was** on Monday.
 It wasn't John **who/that** said that – **it was** me.
 It wasn't a handbag **that** I lost – it **was** a wallet.

4 *Reported questions*
 'Where have you been?'
 She **asked me** where **I had been.**
 'When are you going to arrive?'
 They **wanted to know** when he **was going to** arrive.

Activities

PHOTOGRAPHS

---

1 Look at the first photograph, and answer your teacher's questions about it.

1

2

2 Work in pairs.

Student A: You are going to ask Student B about one of the other
photographs. Prepare three types of question:
1 questions about the photograph itself
2 other questions connected with the photograph
3 questions about related topics
Then interview Student B about the photograph.

Student B: Student A is going to ask you about one of the photographs.
While he is preparing his questions, think about the photograph.
Then answer Student A's questions.

COMPOSITION

Write 120–180 words about one of the following topics:
1 Cars
2 Summer and winter
3 City centres

SITUATIONS

1 You are going to a restaurant less than a kilometre from where you live. A friend
suggests going by car. What might you reply?
2 Your brother has just told you that Maria is ill in hospital, but you saw her shopping
this morning. Explain that he is mistaken.
3 A friend says 'I'm thinking of buying a tumble-drier'. Give him/her some advice.
4 You have to go and see the Principal of your school/college. When you come out a
friend says 'What did he ask you?' Tell your friend.
5 A friend asks you 'What are the advantages of having a credit card?' What do you reply?
6 Your flatmate says to you 'Bill's coming to supper tonight, isn't he?' Correct him/her.
7 An elderly relative tells you 'I'm older than you, so my advice is worth listening to'.
Disagree with him/her, giving your reasons.

Unit 10 Wishes and regrets

10.1 I WISH & IF ONLY

Presentation

I wish a policeman would come along.
If only they would stop following me.

I wish I could telephone the police.
If only I could open this door.

I wish there was a telephone near here.
If only I was 20 years younger.
I wish they didn't have those knives.

1 Why does the man say 'I wish a policeman would come along', and not 'I hope a policeman comes along'?

2 What is the difference between the three sets of remarks above?

3 For each of the following situations, make sentences with **I wish/If only**, using (a) **would**, (b) **could** and (c) **the past tense**.

It's raining.
You're lonely.
You're ill in bed.
Your car's broken down.
You're short of money.

Practice

Look at the pictures below. What do you think the people in them might be thinking? Make sentences using **I wish/If only**.

10.2 CONFLICTING WISHES   Practice

Example: A has a car; B doesn't have a car.

> A: I wish I had a car.
> B: Really? Why's that?
> A: Well, if I had a car, I wouldn't have to spend all my time waiting for buses.
> B: Well, frankly, I wish I didn't have a car.
> A: Really? Why's that?
> B: Because if I didn't have a car, I wouldn't have to take the children to school at seven every morning.

Work in pairs. Have similar conversations, based on the situations below.
1 A doesn't have a telephone; B has a telephone.
2 A doesn't work in London; B works in London.
3 A's children go to boarding school; B's children don't go to boarding school.
4 A's mother hardly ever visits him; B's mother often visits him.
5 A isn't famous; B is famous.
6 A has got a cold; B hasn't got a cold.

10.3 FANTASIES

Free practice [cassette]

You will hear some people answering the question 'If you could spend a day anywhere in the world you wanted to, where would you choose and what would you do there?'

Listen to the tape and answer the questions.
1 What answers did the people give?
2 Which of the people would you most like to accompany?

Work in groups.

Student A: Interview the other people in your group about one of the questions below.

The others: Answer Student A's questions.

1 If you could spend a day anywhere in the world you wanted to, where would you choose and what would you do there?

2 If you had unlimited money to build a house, where would you build it and what would it be like?

3 If you could be in charge of any organisation you liked, which organisation would you choose and how would you run it differently?

Writing

Write a paragraph about one of the topics you discussed.

10.4 REGRET

Presentation and practice

Read the passage below and answer the questions.

James didn't know much about the stock market when he invested all his savings in silver. Shortly afterwards, silver collapsed and he lost all his money. He decided to 'borrow' some money from his company's safe, and use it to win back what he had lost. He knew that he would have to return the money he had taken before the company's accounts were checked on Friday afternoon. On Wednesday evening he took the money to the Casino and lost it all. On Thursday, in desperation, he asked his bank manager for a loan, but the bank manager refused. So when the accounts were checked on Friday, the loss was noticed, and James was arrested for embezzlement. He is now awaiting trial . . .

1 James **regrets not** finding out about the stock market before investing his savings. He **regrets** investing his savings in silver.

What other things does he regret doing/not doing?

2 James: 'I **wish I'd** known more / **should've** found out more about the stock market. If I'd known more about the stock market, I would never have invested my savings in silver.'

What else might he say? Make sentences with
a) I wish . . . hadn't . . .
b) I should(n't) have . . .
c) If . . .

10.5   FEELING SORRY FOR YOURSELF   Practice

What might you regret in these situations, using **I wish .../If only ...** or **I shouldn't ...**?

1 You're suffering from sunstroke.
2 War has suddenly broken out, and you're stuck in your hotel room.
3 Your house has burnt down.
4 You feel seasick.
5 You're short of sleep.
6 Someone has just refused to marry you.
7 You're stuck half way up a mountain in fog.

Work in pairs. Have conversations as in the example.

A: | I wish I'd sat in the shade.
   | I should never have taken the roof off the car.

B: Why/Why not?

A: Because | if I'd sat in the shade | I wouldn't have got so burnt.
           | if I hadn't taken it off |

10.6   I WISH I'D KNOWN: READING GAME   Practice

Work in groups of three. You are students A, B, and C.
Read through your own section only, and then play the game, starting with Student A.

Example   (You didn't tell me the buses were running)
       A: **I wish** you'd told me the buses were running ...

       (I didn't go by bus)
B or C: **I could have** gone by bus.
or
       (I walked all that way)
B or C: **I needn't have** walked all that way.

Student A
Read out sentences 1–4 using **I wish/If only**.
Students B and C will continue them.

1 I didn't know the lecture had been cancelled:
2 You didn't tell me they were on the telephone:
3 I didn't realise that book was in the library:
4 Nobody told me he was a vegetarian:

Choose one of these sentences to continue what B and C read out. Change each one to include either **could have** or **needn't have**.

. . . I didn't lend you mine.
. . . I brought the car.
. . . I got changed.
. . . We didn't get a taxi.
. . . I didn't come round for a game of cards.
. . . I hired one.
. . . I brought my own.
. . . We didn't have a game of doubles.

Student B
Read out sentences 1–4 using **I wish/If only**.
Students A and C will continue them.

1 I didn't realise it was so near:
2 Nobody told me food would be provided:
3 You didn't tell me you had any money:
4 You didn't mention that your friends played tennis:

Choose one of these sentences to continue what A and C read out. Change each one to include either **could have** or **needn't have**.

. . . I didn't come round for a game of cards.
. . . I didn't make an omelette.
. . . I hired one.
. . . I went all the way to their house.
. . . I bought a copy.
. . . I got changed.
. . . I didn't stay at home.
. . . I didn't lend you mine.

Student C
Read out sentences 1–4 using **I wish/If only**.
Students A and B will continue them.

1 I didn't realise you were on your own:
2 You didn't say you had a typewriter:
3 I didn't know it would be such an informal party:
4 You didn't tell me you'd lost your umbrella:

Choose one of these sentences to continue what A and B read out. Change each one to include either **could have** or **needn't have**.

. . . I bought a copy.
. . . I didn't stay at home.
. . . We didn't have a game of doubles.
. . . I brought my own.
. . . I didn't make an omelette.
. . . I brought the car.
. . . I went all the way to their house.
. . . We didn't get a taxi.

10.7   WISHES AND REGRETS

Free practice

Interview two *different* people in the class. Take notes during each interview.

Interview 1: Wishes
Find out from the person you interview what occupation he (or she) wishes he had instead of his present one.
Find out:

1 what occupation
2 why he wishes he had it
3 why he can't/doesn't have it
4 whether he thinks he ever will

Interview 2: Regrets
Find out from the person you interview any hobbies/sports he (or she) wishes he had taken up when he was younger.
Find out:

1 what hobbies/sports
2 why he wishes he'd taken them up
3 why he never did take them up
4 if he thinks he ever will

Writing

From your notes, write two paragraphs about the wishes and regrets of the two people you interviewed.

10.8   CHILDREN'S WISHES   Reading

Read these paragraphs, which were all written by English schoolchildren, and answer the questions.

I wish I was a lion. I could rule the whole jungle. Monkeys, tigers, and giraffes would look up to me. I would have a long shaggy mane, and a wife and children. My sleek coat would be no trouble at all. I wouldn't have to bother about school and lessons, I would know it all from birth. I would have my den in the best place and I would chose who came to call.
Marian

I wish I hadn't got three sisters who are very boring and I haven't got a brother to play with only girls. *Adam*

I wish I hadn't got my dress dirty yesterday Then I shouldn't have had to wear this dress today.
Rachel

I wish that I was a cat. Cats
are much more intelligent than
humans, they don't go to school.
If I was a cat, I would be able to
look at everyone as if I was were
their master and they had to
obey my every wish. All afternoon,
I would cat-nap in a tree dream
-ing of   fish, and
what else cats dream of. At
supper time I would dash into
the house, and meow loudly
until my master fed me. After that,
I would go back to sleep till the
next day.

Vincent

I wish I hadn't got to go to
school. I wanted to go to a
convent and now go to boarding
school. September and gloves for
hats mum told me I have to
uniform wear ally school
wish

Sarah

I wish that school holidays would
never end, so I could get away from
all the maths and "history ect, I would
not have to keep saying "Yes sir! No sir!".
If this were possible I would go to
the cinema when ever want to.

Ian

I wish I had a trick stick
So I could swing it a
round my head. *Anne-Marie*

I wish that we did not have
to buy things with money it would
be much easier not to bother, just think
of what you could do you could
go into a shop wich sells very
expensive clothes and take every thing
that fits you, or take all of
your favourite sweets at the sweet
shop, would'nt that be just marvellous.

Liza

I wish I hadn't hgot a
trick stick then I wouldn't
have a bruise on my
hhead. *Alana*

⋙→

1 Which of the paragraphs express *regret*?
2 What do you think a 'trick stick' is? (Anne-Marie and Alana)
3 What doesn't Rachel like about her present situation?
4 Explain the following:
   a) cat-nap; dash (Vincent)
   b) boarding school; convent (Sarah)
   c) shaggy mane; sleek coat; den (Marian)
5 Which paragraph do you find the most imaginative? Why?
6 How old do you think each of the children is?
7 What mistakes can you find in the paragraphs?

Unit 10   *Summary of language*

In this unit, you have learnt how to:
– wish for changes
– express dissatisfaction with your present situation
– imagine yourself differently
– express regret

KEY POINTS

1 *I wish/If only*
   I wish someone **would** help me.
   If only I **could** read the sign.

   I wish they lived nearer.
   I wish I **wasn't** so tired.

   If only I'd gone to bed earlier.
   I wish I **hadn't** spent so much money.

2 *Conditional structures*
   If I could read the sign, **I'd** know which way to go.
   If they lived nearer, we **could** see each other every day.
   If I'd gone to bed earlier, **I wouldn't have** overslept.
   If I hadn't spent so much money, **I'd be able** to get a taxi home.

3 *Should have done*
   I should have gone to bed earlier.
   I shouldn't have spent so much money.

4 *Could/Needn't have done*
   I wish you'd told me you were going to the post office – **I needn't have** gone myself.
   I wish I'd realised you were short of money – **I could have** lent you some.

Activities

JUNG'S DREAM

Here is an account of a dream by the psychologist Carl Jung:

I was in a house I did not know, although I felt it was 'my house'. I found myself in the upper storey, where there was a kind of salon with fine old furniture in early eighteenth century style. I was surprised that this should be my house, and thought, 'Not bad'. But then it occurred to me that I didn't know what the lower floor looked like, so I went downstairs. There everything was much older, and I realised that this part of the house must date from about the fifteenth century. Everywhere it was rather dark. I went from one room to another thinking, 'Now I really must explore the whole house'. I came upon a heavy door, and opened it. Beyond it I discovered a stone stairway that led down into the cellar. At the bottom, I found myself in a beautiful vaulted room that looked extremely ancient. I looked at the walls, and realised they dated from Roman times. The floor was made of stone slabs, and in one of these I discovered a ring. When I pulled it, the stone slab lifted, and again I saw a stairway of narrow stone steps leading down to the depths. These too I descended, and entered a low cave cut into the rock. Thick dust lay on the floor, and in the dust were bones and broken pottery, like the remains of a very primitive culture. I discovered two human skulls, obviously very old and half disintegrated. Then I woke up.

1. a) What, if anything, do you think the dream might mean?
   b) What do you think particular things in the dream might represent, for example: the house; the different floors, each darker and older than the last; the human skulls.

2 a) Do you think dreams do have any symbolic significance?
  b) Have you ever had a dream that you think 'means something'?

COMPOSITION

Write 120–180 words on one of the following:
1 Give your own explanation of the meaning of Jung's dream.
2 Tell the story of a dream you have had.

Unit 11   Events in sequence

Look at these two series of events, and answer the questions.

Story A   Richard opened the cupboard.
He saw a spider.
He screamed.
His mother heard him.
She ran into the room.
He told her about the spider.
She couldn't help laughing.

Story B   Richard's mother gave him his supper.
Then she tucked him into bed.
Then she read him a story.
Then she kissed him goodnight.
Then she put out the light.
Then she went downstairs.
Then he started crying.

1 Join each pair of events in Stories A and B using **When** ...
2 In which story could we use **After** ... instead of **When** ... ?

Now change the following sentences, using **When** instead of **and** or **but**.
1   She peeled the banana and gave it to the baby.
2   I looked in the fridge and found some sausages.
3   The security men searched our hand baggage and we boarded the plane.
4   He kicked the dog and it barked.
5   I went to the duty free shop and bought a carton of Gauloises.
6   The plane took off and the stewardess came round with orange juice.
7   He drank the coffee and asked for another cup.
8   I paid my bill and left the restaurant.
9   He put his foot on the brake but nothing happened.
10   I read the letter and threw it into the wastepaper basket.
11   I read his autobiography and discovered what a strange person he had been.

11.2 AS SOON AS   Practice

Examples I recognised you **as soon as** I **heard** your voice.
            As soon as they **had moved in** they gave a house-warming party.

In the same way, change the sentences below, using
either: **as soon as** + Past
or: **as soon as** + Past Perfect

1 They saw the house and immediately fell in love with it.
2 I wrote the letter and posted it straight away.
3 He got his exam results and immediately rang up his parents.
4 The train passed and immediately the crossing barrier went up.
5 He got married again immediately after his wife's death.
6 He left the house straight after breakfast.
7 I looked into her eyes and knew immediately that she was the girl for me.
8 I told him about my problem and he instantly offered to help.
9 The television programme finished and then I went straight to bed.

11.3 WHAT HAPPENED? READING GAME   Practice

Work in groups of three. You are students A, B, and C.
Read through your own section only, and then play the game, starting with
Student A.

Example A: When the burglar opened the safe . . .
           B or C: . . . the alarm went off.

           A: When the burglar had opened the safe . . .
           B or C: . . . he filled his bag with money.

Student A

Read out each of these sentences twice:
a) beginning **When** / **As soon as** + Past
b) beginning **When** / **As soon as** + Past Perfect

Students B and C will continue them.

1 He took off his shoes and socks . . .
2 The doctor gave me an injection . . .
3 I lit the gas . . .

Choose one from each of these pairs of sentences to continue what B and C read out.

. . . I got dressed.
. . . my legs gave way under me.

. . . I gave him a big tip.
. . . I carried my suitcase into the hotel.

. . . he rewound it and played it again.
. . . he got a splitting headache.

. . . I realised they'd given me £5 too much.
. . . I put it in my pocket.

. . . I found a cheque for £5000 inside.
. . . I took out the letter and read it.

. . . I felt the earth move under my feet.
. . . I went into the bathroom to wipe the lipstick off my face.

Student B

Read out each of these sentences twice:
a) beginning **When** / **As soon as** + Past
b) beginning **When** / **As soon as** + Past Perfect

Students A and C will continue them.

1 I opened the envelope . . .
2 He listened to the tape . . .
3 I paid the taxi driver . . .

Choose one from each of these pairs of sentences to continue what A and C read out.

. . . we all nearly suffocated from the smell.
. . . he got up and waded into the water.

. . . I went into the bathroom to wipe the lipstick off my face.
. . . I felt the earth move under my feet.

. . . I put it in my pocket.
. . . I realised they'd given me £5 too much.

. . . there was a big explosion.
. . . I put the kettle on.

. . . he wrote me a prescription.
. . . I felt a sharp pain in my arm.

. . . my legs gave way under me.
. . . I got dressed.

Student C

Read out each of these sentences twice:
a) beginning **When** / **As soon as** + Past
b) beginning **When** / **As soon as** + Past Perfect

Students A and B will continue them.

1 I counted my change . . .
2 She kissed me . . .
3 I got out of bed . . .

Choose one from each of these pairs of sentences to continue what A and B read out.

. . . he got a splitting headache.
. . . he rewound it and played it again.

. . . I put the kettle on.
. . . there was a big explosion.

. . . I felt a sharp pain in my arm.
. . . he wrote me a prescription.

. . . I gave him a big tip.
. . . I carried my suitcase into the hotel.

. . . we all nearly suffocated from the smell.
. . . he got up and waded into the water.

. . . I took out the letter and read it.
. . . I found a cheque for £5000 inside.

SWITCH OFF THE MAINS FIRST!

RIGHT **WRONG**

Examples: *turned off the mains / touched the wire*
    A: He turned off the mains **before he touched** the wire.
    B: He **didn't** touch the wire **until he'd turned** off the mains.
    C: He got the job done.

    touched the wire / turned off the mains
    A: He **didn't** turn off the mains **before he touched** the wire.
    B: He touched the wire **before he'd turned off** the mains.
    C: He was electrocuted.

Work in threes. Look at the pairs of actions below, and for each pair:
a) decide whether the person did things in the right order
b) say what happened as a result

1 resigned / found another job
2 checked his change / left the shop
3 started driving the car / insured it
4 signed the contract / read it
5 had a good breakfast / set out
6 fastened her seat belt / drove off
7 bought the shoes / tried them on
8 wiped his feet / came in

Now tell the others about an occasion when you did something in the wrong order. Say what you did wrong, and what happened.

11.5 SUCCESS STORY

Free practice

Work in pairs.

Pair A: You have *either* organised a successful music festival
                or set up a small but successful package tour company.
         Decide how you got the idea, what different things you had to do to get
         started, and why you think you were successful.

Pair B: You have *either* opened a very successful and fashionable boutique
                or organised a successful sporting event.
         Decide how you got the idea, what different things you had to do to get
         started, and why you think you were successful.

         Now form new pairs (one A and one B) and interview each other about
         what you did.

Writing

Write a paragraph telling either your own or the other person's success story.

11.6 UNEXPECTED EVENTS

Presentation and practice

Example

> # Bomb attack: President leaves palace just in time

The President **had only just left** the Palace **when** a bomb exploded in his office.

No sooner had the President left the Palace **than** a bomb exploded in his office.

Explain the newspaper headlines below in the same way
a) using ... **had only just...** **when** ...
b) using **No sooner had** ... **than** ...

1 Peace talks break down on first day
2 *Manchester player breaks leg in first minute of match*
3 **New king abdicates**
4 **Jewel thief caught red-handed**
5 **Missing first husband ruins honeymoon**
6 **New casino destroyed in blaze**
7 **Tanker sinks on maiden voyage**

Practice

Example: He reached his house ...

| He had only just reached his house when | there was a loud clap of thunder |
| No sooner had he reached his house than | and it started pouring with rain. |

Develop the sentences below in the same way. Each one should describe a *narrow escape*.

1 The audience came out of the cinema ...
2 I reached the shore ...
3 I left the island ...
4 I changed all my dollars into sterling ...
5 We got the harvest in ...
6 She insured the painting ...
7 I sold my house ...

11.7 TELLING A STORY

Free practice

Philip had dinner
and went to the
pub ...

As soon as Philip came home from work, he cooked himself some
dinner. When he had finished eating, he decided to go to the pub and see
some friends. The pub was almost empty when he arrived, since it was
still early.

... He watched a
football match on
the pub TV ...

He'd only been there a
few minutes when the
landlord turned on the
TV for the big football
match. Philip decided to
stay and watch it.

Continue the story, using the notes below to help you. Fill in any details you
like, paying special attention to the order in which events happened.

... Then the news came on. ...

... A house was on fire ...

... Philip remembered the pan of oil. ...

... He rushed home ...

Work in groups. Each set of notes below gives the beginning of a story. Tell two of the stories, making them up as you go along. Work round the group (Student A, then B, then C . . .), adding a few sentences each.

1 Marilyn took some rubbish out to the dustbin . . .
   . . . The front door slammed shut . . .

2 The Thompsons went for a drive in the country . . .
   . . . There was a terrible thunderstorm . . .

3 Diana's marriage broke up . . .
   . . . She decided to emigrate to Australia . . .

4 Jim asked Rhoda out to dinner . . .
   . . . Rhoda didn't turn up at the restaurant . . .

Writing

Write one of the stories you told.

11.8 TWIN STORIES

Listening 📼

You will hear two stories about
Don Binney and his brother Ken.
Work in groups.

Group A: Listen to the first story, and answer the questions.
  1 What period of the speaker's life is he talking about?
  2 Where were (a) the speaker? (b) his brother?
  3 What was unusual about the speaker and his brother?
  4 a) Why did the speaker want to have his photo taken?
     b) Describe the photo.
  5 What did Ken do with the photo, and how was he able to do this?
  6 a) The squadron leader accused Ken of doing two things. What were they?
     b) Why does the speaker say the second accusation was 'absolutely ridiculous'?
  7 What punishment was Ken given?

Group B: Listen to the second story, and answer the questions.
  1 What period of the speaker's life is he talking about?
  2 At the beginning of the story, where were (a) the speaker? (b) his brother?
  3 What was unusual about the speaker and his brother?
  4 Make a list of the main things the speaker did in the story.
  5 Two people had used the taxi just before the speaker. Who were they?
  6 a) Where did the speaker get his suntan?
     b) Why did his suntan confuse the taxi driver?

Now form pairs (one A and one B), and tell each other the stories you have
heard.

Writing

Write either the first or the second story.

Unit 11   Summary of language

In this unit, you have learnt how to:
– talk about the sequence of past events
– talk about unexpected events in the past

KEY POINTS

1 *'When' and 'After'*
   When I read the letter I was horrified.
   When the telephone **rang**, he answered it.

   When/After I'd read his letter I put it in my pocket.
   When/After I'd bought my ticket, I went and had some coffee.

2 *'As soon as'*
   As soon as the telephone **rang**, he answered it.
   As soon as I'd bought my ticket, I went and had some coffee.

3 *Emphasising the right order*
   Fortunately, he insured his luggage **before** he sent it.
   He **didn't** send his luggage **until** he'd insured it.
   Unfortunately, he **didn't** read the contract **before** he signed it.
   He signed the contract **before** he'd read it.

4 *Unexpected events*
   The plane **had only just** taken off **when** the engines failed.
   No sooner had the plane taken off **than** the engines failed.

Activities

Student A:
You: live in a large house in the suburbs
have an important job in the Civil Service
drive a Mercedes
have a holiday cottage by the sea
have four children
You are not very satisfied with your life-style. You don't know B very well, but you think his/her life-style must be much more enjoyable and satisfying.
Imagine the advantages of B's life-style, and think of the disadvantages of your own.

Student B:
You: share a flat in the city centre
work as a freelance photographer
have several girl/boyfriends
ride a motorbike
travel to many countries in connection with your work
You are not very satisfied with your life-style. You don't know A very well, but you think his/her life-style must be much more enjoyable and satisfying.
Imagine the advantages of A's life-style, and think of the disadvantages of your own.

Now form new pairs (one A and one B), and discuss your life-styles.

COMPOSITION

Write 120–180 words on one of the topics below:
1 Happiness
2 Jealousy
3 Habits

Unit 12   Comparison

12.1   LARGE AND SMALL DIFFERENCES

Presentation and practice

A travel magazine recently sent two of its reporters on different coach tours to the Costa Brava. Here are parts of their reports:

PARADISE HOLIDAYS	15 days: £295

The coach was brand new, but the windows were filthy and the floor was covered with rubbish from the last tour. Our courier, Sandra, got us off on time and there were no delays on the journey there or back. Sandra spoke fluent Spanish, and was obviously an old hand at this particular tour. On the whole, she didn't socialise much with the group, but did manage to sort out any problem as it arose. The hotel was comfortable, and about 3 km. from the beach, and the food was good and well cooked – I did, however, find myself buying extra snacks now and then. I found the excursions rather expensive (about £12 a time) but there were plenty of them, and lots of choice.

VISTA TOURS	14 days: £199

The coach, though old and needing a service, was spotlessly clean, and when we eventually got away the journey was quite pleasant. Our courier, Geoff, had only done this run once before, and his Spanish was a bit shaky, but he was great fun: he was never away from the group, and really tried his best (which was not always good enough!) to keep things going smoothly. We arrived at last at the hotel, which I found quite comfortable, apart from the mattress. The food was nice, but not always as hot as it could have been – and there was usually enough of it. The beach was only about three or four minutes' walk away, and if one got bored with that, one could go on a local excursion – reasonable at about £9.50 a time, but not as much choice as I'd been hoping for.

Paradise Holidays are **much** more expensive than Vista Tours.
Paradise Holidays last **a little** longer than Vista Tours.

1   What words could replace (a) **much** (b) **a little** in the sentences above?

2   From the information in the reports, make other comparisons between the two tours. Talk about:
   a)   The coaches. How old? Clean?
   b)   The couriers. Efficient? Spanish? Experience? Friendly?
   c)   The hotel. Comfort? Near to beach?
   d)   The food. Quality? Quantity?
   e)   The excursions. Cost? Choice?
   f)   The tours. Well organised? Good? Good value for money?

3   Now compare the two tours as in the examples below.
   Examples   Vista Tours are**n't nearly as** expensive as Paradise Holidays.
   Vista Tours don't last **quite as** long as Paradise Holidays.
   Vista Tours last **almost/nearly as** long as Paradise Holidays.

Writing

Write a paragraph comparing Paradise Holidays and Vista Tours. Say which you would rather go on, and why.

12.2 SIMILARITIES AND DIFFERENCES   Free practice

Work in pairs. Discuss the ways in which you and your partner are similar and different. Talk about the topics below, and use the expressions you learnt in 12.1.

physical appearance and dress   accommodation
skills and leisure activities   work and routine

Now tell someone else how similar/different you and your partner are.

12.3 COMPARING PRICES   Presentation and practice

Compare the prices of steak and chicken, beginning:
a) Steak is about three times . . .
b) Steak costs about three times . . .
c) Chicken is about a third . . .

Compare the prices of the things below in the same way:
1 tinned peas: 25p   frozen peas: 48p
2 cotton sheets: £14   silk sheets: £150
3 olive oil: £2   corn oil: 99p
4 leather gloves: £8   woollen gloves: £2.75
5 colour TV: £310   black-and-white TV: £60

Work in pairs. Have conversations, as in the example.

A: Which shall I get, steak or chicken?

B: | Don't get steak. It's far more expensive than chicken.
    | Get chicken. It's far cheaper than steak.

A: | How much more?
    | How much cheaper?

B: Oh, it's about | three times the price.
                   | a third of the price.

1 Write the other nouns in the table.

expensive   *price* ....

deep   ....

high/tall   ....

wide   ....

thick   ....

long   ....

heavy   ....

fast   ....

2 Compare the things below in as many different ways as you can.
   Example   The Rolls Royce is probably about 20 times the price
             of the Mini Metro.

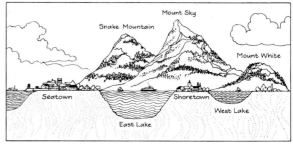

You will hear three people playing a game in which two of them are trying to guess the name of an object. Listen to the tape and answer the questions.

1 What is the object?
2 How is it similar to/different from the objects in the list below?
   a postcard
   a refrigerator
   a packet of cigarettes
   a ruler
   a football
   an LP record
   a flower pot

Work in groups.

Student A: Write down the name of a common object, and tell the others *only* what it's made of.

The others: Try to guess what the object is by asking questions which refer to the list. You can ask two kinds of questions:
   a) Comparison questions:
      e.g. How heavy is it compared to an LP record?
           Would I use it as often as I use a refrigerator?
   b) Similarity questions:
      e.g. Does it have a similar shape to a flower pot?

12.6 COMPARISONS WITH DIFFERENT TENSES   Presentation and practice

It isn't as warm today as	it was yesterday.
	the weather forecast said it would be.
	it ought to be at this time of year.
	I thought it would be.

They gave us far less food than	we'd expected them to.
	they should have done.
	they'd said they would.
	they usually do.

Make similar comparisons, beginning with the words below:

1 I'm much happier here ...
2 There weren't nearly as many people ...
3 They go out far more often ...
4 She didn't dance as well ...

Now change these sentences below into comparative sentences using: (a) **than** (b) **as ... as.**

1 The exam is not usually very difficult, but this year it was quite tough.
2 I had imagined my landlady would be in her fifties, but she turned out to be thirty.
3 His parents would like him to work hard, but he doesn't.
4 The washing machine makes a lot of noise, although it used to be fairly quiet.
5 You said I would enjoy the film, but in fact I didn't like it much.
6 I had hoped to do quite a lot of work today, but I've only managed to do a little.
7 They could have helped me a lot, but in fact they hardly helped me at all.
8 I hadn't expected her to be very angry, but in fact she was absolutely furious.
9 Fifty people had been invited, but eighty came.

12.7 NOT WHAT I'D EXPECTED

Free practice

Teacher: 'Soon after I started teaching maths, I discovered that it was far harder work than I'd expected it to be. I'd imagined I would have plenty of time to myself (after all, I was officially working far fewer hours than I had been in my previous job) – but instead I found myself working late every evening just to prepare for the next day's classes. But it was also a lot more satisfying than I'd imagined it would be ...'

Work in groups. Tell the others about one of the following:
1 A place you visited that was very different from what you'd expected.
2 Someone you met who was different from what you'd imagined him/her to be like.
3 A disappointing experience you had.
4 An experience you had that was unexpectedly pleasant.

Writing

Write a paragraph describing either the story you told or one of the stories you heard.

Reading

There is only one way to gain weight – and that is to eat or drink more calories than you can use up in energy every day. There is only one way to lose weight – to eat fewer calories than you use up in energy every day.

Fats are the highest calorie foods of all – twice as high in calories as sugary and starchy carbohydrates. The calorie chart below shows how disproportionately high in calories fats are compared with other everyday foods. Compare 100 calories for a 112 gram portion of potatoes to 205 calories for the same potatoes with a 15 gram knob of butter. By giving up the butter, you will make a significant reduction in your calories without reducing the bulk of what you eat.

Butter, margarine and cooking or salad oils are all easily identified as fats, but many fats are 'invisible'. Unseen by the eye, they nevertheless exist in many foods to make a high-calorie contribution to your diet. This particularly applies to protein foods, many of which are much higher in fat content than they appear. Tongue, for example, has a much higher invisible fat content than chicken, and this is reflected in tongue having twice as many calories.

Changing from high-fat foods to low-fat foods is often effortless. Yet the saving in calories can be very great. The calorie cost of 85 gm of roast chicken, for example, is only 125, whereas an equivalent portion of Cheddar cheese comes to 360 calories. Let's take a typical day's menu from a do-it-yourself slimmer, which seems, at first glance, to be 'virtuous'.

Breakfast:
    Two slices buttered toast (no jam, no marmalade).
    Two cups tea or coffee (no sugar).
Lunch:
    Cheese omelette and dressed salad.
Dinner:
    115 gm paté, with two slices buttered bread.
    ¼ litre milk in tea and coffee.

The fat content of a 'modest' menu like this comes to more than 200 grams. This means that even though this slimmer has taken very little food, 2,175 calories have been consumed.

The average woman needs only 2,000 calories a day, and the average man about 500 calories more. In this case, our Mrs Average, in spite of eating very little, has taken in 175 calories more than her body needs. Even this small number of excess calories eaten daily could add up to an increase in weight of 8 kilos in a year.

		Calories (per 28 gm)		Calories (per 28 gm)
Some fats	Butter	210	Olive oil	255
	Margarine	210	Corn oil	255
Some high-carbohydrate foods	Potatoes	25	Flour	100
	Bread	65	Sugar	110
Some fatty high-protein foods	Tongue	85	Roast breast of lamb	115
	Cheddar cheese	120		
Some low-fat protein foods	Cod or haddock fillet (not fried)	22	Roast chicken (skinned)	42
Some fruit and vegetables	Melon	4	Orange	7
	Mushrooms	4	Eating apple	10
	Cabbage	6	Peas	15

Now compare the above menu with a typical day's menu followed by a slimmer who is on a low-fat diet.

Breakfast:
   Two fish-cakes, grilled.
   Tomatoes.
   225 gm baked beans.
Lunch:
   Vegetable omelette (two eggs, 50 gm
      mixed vegetables), cooked with 7 gm
      low-fat margarine.
   Salad or extra vegetables.
   Piece of fresh fruit.
Dinner:
   150gm Campbell's Bolognese Sauce.
   1 cup boiled spaghetti.
   Fresh fruit salad.
   1 small natural yoghurt.

Because of the low amount of fat in the menu, this slimmer consumes only 1000 calories.

(Adapted from *Dieting Revolution*, published by Slimming magazine)

1 How do people gain and lose weight?
2 What is special about fats compared to other foods?
3 What are 'invisible' fats? Why are they important?
4 a) Why does the do-it-yourself slimmer's diet seem 'virtuous'?
   b) Why isn't it effective?
5 Make sentences comparing the number of calories in:
   a) butter and flour
   b) tongue and chicken
   c) flour and sugar
   d) Cheddar cheese and chicken
   e) mushrooms and margarine
6 Make comparisons between the menus of the do-it-yourself slimmer and the low-fat slimmer.
7 According to the writer, what is the main advantage of a low-fat diet compared with other types of diet?

Discussion

1 Does any of the information given in the passage surprise you?
2 Why do you think men, on average, need to consume more calories than women?
3 Have you ever been on a diet? What sort of diet? What happened?
4 a) What alternatives are there to a low-fat diet for people who want to lose weight?
   b) How would you try to lose weight?

Writing

A friend has written to you, saying he/she is on a strict diet and is eating very little, but that he/she is still putting on weight.
Write a reply (about 150 words), explaining what he/she is doing wrong and giving some good advice.

Unit 12   Summary of language

In this unit, you have learnt how to:
– talk about large and small differences
– make precise comparisons
– make comparisons involving different times
– compare the way things are with what you expected

KEY POINTS

1 *Large and small differences*
   He works **much** harder **than** I do.
   Beef is **slightly more** expensive **than** lamb.
   I don't work **nearly as** hard **as** he does.
   Lamb is **almost as** expensive **as** beef.

2 *Numerical comparisons*
   Real leather is three times | **as** expensive **as** / **the** price **of** | imitation leather.

   Birmingham is about twice | **as** big **as** / **the** size **of** | Liverpool.

   Liverpool is about half | **as** big **as** / **the** size **of** | Birmingham.

3 *Comparisons with different tenses*
   I **know** far more people than I **did** a year ago.
   They **don't play** as well as they **used to**.
   The car **used** up more petrol than it **should have done**.
   The problem **was** more difficult than **I'd expected** (it to be).
   I **didn't get** quite as much money as **I'd thought** I would.

Activities

QUIZ

You are going to take part in a quiz. The quiz will test your general knowledge and your knowledge of English.

COMPOSITION

Write 120–180 words on one of these topics:
1 A magazine has asked its readers for their views on astrology. Write to the magazine expressing your opinions.
2 Write a review for a newspaper of a recent film, play or book.
3 You recently bought *either* a car *or* a washing machine *or* a TV. You've had a lot of trouble with it ever since you bought it, and the after-sales service has been very unsatisfactory. Finally you write a letter to the radio programme 'Any Complaints?', telling them about your problem.

SITUATIONS

1 You're feeling depressed. Make a wish.
2 A friend isn't sure whether to buy local or imported beer. Tell him/her which to buy, and why.
3 You had an accident while doing an electrical repair, and are now in hospital. Explain to a visitor exactly what you did wrong.
4 You've just come back from a disappointing holiday. Tell a friend how it was different from what you'd expected.
5 You changed jobs recently, and now you regret it. Express your regret, and explain why.
6 The other day you narrowly escaped being run over. Say what happened.
7 Last week a friend forgot to tell you that a football match had been cancelled. When you see him/her, you complain. What do you say?

Unit 13   Processes

Presentation and practice

Look at the two sets of sentences below, which are about mousetraps. What is
the difference between the two sets?

First you cut off a piece of cheese.
When you've cut off the cheese,
    you place it in the trap.
When you've placed it in the trap,
    you set the spring.

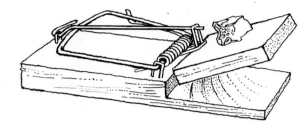

When the mouse smells the cheese,
    it goes up to it and starts eating it.
When it moves the cheese, it
    releases the spring.
When the spring is released, the
    bar snaps over and traps the
    mouse.

Look at the prompts below and
a) join them using **When** . . .
b) add another sentence beginning with **When** . . . saying what you do next.

1 arrive/border →   show/passport →
2 water/boil →   pour/teapot →
3 turn off/light →   change/bulb →
4 turn on/gas →   light/gas →
5 meet/stranger →   shake/hands →
6 eat/meal →   pay/bill →

Practice

Work in groups.
a) Make a list of what is involved in the following processes.
b) Talk about each process using **When** ...

1 crossing the road
2 using a public telephone box
3 mending a bicycle puncture

13.2   EMPHASISING THE RIGHT ORDER   Practice

Example: *cross the road / look both ways*
>   A: You should look both ways **before** you **cross** the road ...
>   B: You should**n't** cross the road **before/until** you've looked both
>   ways ...
>   C: **Otherwise** you might get run over.

Work in threes. Say what order you should do these things in, and why, as in
the example.
1 wind the film on / close the camera
2 wind the film on / take a picture
3 read the label / wash a blouse
4 change a fuse / turn off the mains
5 pay the bill / check it
6 bandage a wound / clean it
7 listen to the weather forecast / go sailing
8 buy your girlfriend a ring / ask her to marry you

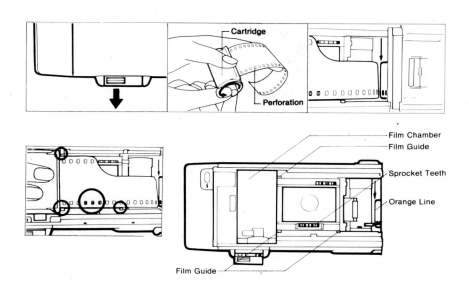

13.3 GIVING INSTRUCTIONS

Free practice 🖭

You will hear someone giving instructions for making coffee. Listen to the tape and answer the questions.

1 What kind of coffee is the speaker talking about?
2 In the space below, make two lists of the stages involved in making the coffee.

Things you do (e.g. turn the gas on)	*Things that happen* (e.g. the water boils)

3 Say exactly how *you* would make coffee.

Work in groups.
1 Talk about something you know how to do which involves doing things in a particular order.
2 Take notes from what other people tell you.

Here are some possible topics:

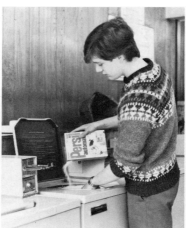

Writing

Write instructions for one of the
processes you've heard about.

13.4 NATURAL PROCESSES Presentation and practice

All the verbs below describe changes of state.
Which of them are used for talking about:

1 changes in size?
2 solids becoming liquid?
3 liquids becoming solid?
4 liquids becoming gas?
5 gases becoming liquid?

set	dissolve	condense
expand	congeal	contract
freeze	melt	shrink
evaporate	stretch	swell

What happens when you . . .
. . . put a lump of ice in a glass of lemonade?
. . . leave a pullover in hot water?
. . . leave liquid cement on the ground?
. . . leave a bowl of water outside in the sun?
. . . leave a bowl of water outside at the South Pole?
. . . leave a bowl of hot water in front of a mirror?
. . . put a lump of sugar in your coffee?
. . . blow into a balloon?
. . . pour cold water onto hot metal?
. . . leave rice in a bowl of water?
. . . fill a bowl with blood and leave it?

Work in groups. You are a panel of experts who write a column called 'Science for Everyone' for a magazine. In your column, you answer readers' questions about science. Discuss how you will answer the following questions which you have received.

1   The lock on my car door was frozen up the other morning, and I couldn't turn the key in it. My next door neighbour advised me to pour a little whisky into the lock. I did this, and it worked. Can you tell me why?
2   Can you tell me why glasses crack when you pour boiling water in them?
3   Please explain how clouds form and why it rains.
4   Why is it that when I get in my car on a cold morning the windows get steamed up?
5   Why do pipes burst in winter?

13.6   THE PASSIVE IN DESCRIBING PROCESSES   Practice

The notes and pictures below illustrate the process of producing and publishing a book. Describe the process in as much detail as you can, using the Passive wherever possible. Begin:

When a couple of sample chapters have been written, they are typed out neatly and sent to the publisher, together with an outline of the rest of the story. This is read by a publisher's reader and the publisher himself . . .

Work in groups. Discuss what stages you think are involved in the processes below.

1 ears of corn → sliced bread

2 writing a letter → reading a letter

3 cow → wallet

13.7   HOW THINGS WORK

Free practice

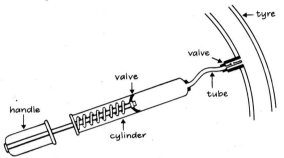

When the handle is pulled out, the valve inside the cylinder opens, and this allows the cylinder to fill with air. As the handle is pushed in, the increased air pressure inside the cylinder closes the valve, and air is forced out of the other end of the cylinder, through the tube, and into the tyre. The air enters the tyre through a valve, which prevents it from escaping from the tyre when the handle is pulled back again.

Look at the example, which explains how a bicycle pump works. In the same way, describe how the things below work.

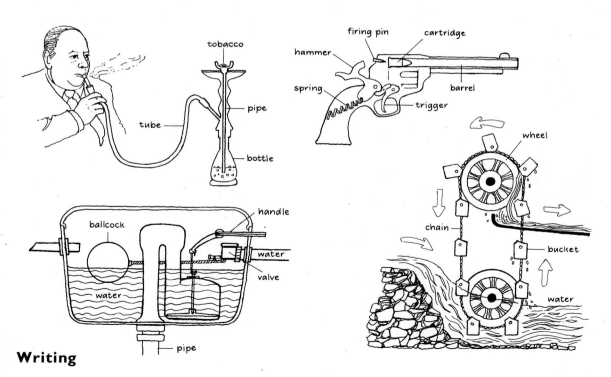

Writing

Choose two of the things above, and write a paragraph explaining how each one works.

13.8 MAKING YOUR OWN WINE

Listening 📼

You will hear somebody being interviewed about making wine at home. Listen to the tape and answer the questions.

PART 1 : STARTING YOUR WINE
1 What is the most important thing to remember when you make your own wine?
2 Make a list of the basic ingredients you need.
3 When you've put your ingredients in the jar, what *two* things do you do?

PART 2 : THE PROCESS OF FERMENTATION
4 What is fermentation?
5 What does the yeast do?

PART 3 : FINISHING YOUR WINE
6 When fermentation has finished, why do you:
   a) add chemicals?
   b) leave the wine for a week?
7 a) How is the wine transferred into a clean jar?
   b) Why is this done?
8 How long do you have to wait before you can drink your wine?

PART 4 : COST AND QUALITY
9 What two advantages are there in making your own wine?
10 What happens at the end of the interview?

Listen to Parts 1–3 again. As you listen, write down in note form exactly what you do at each of the stages shown below.

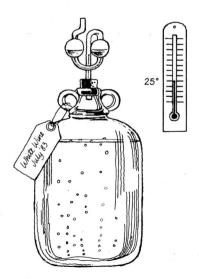

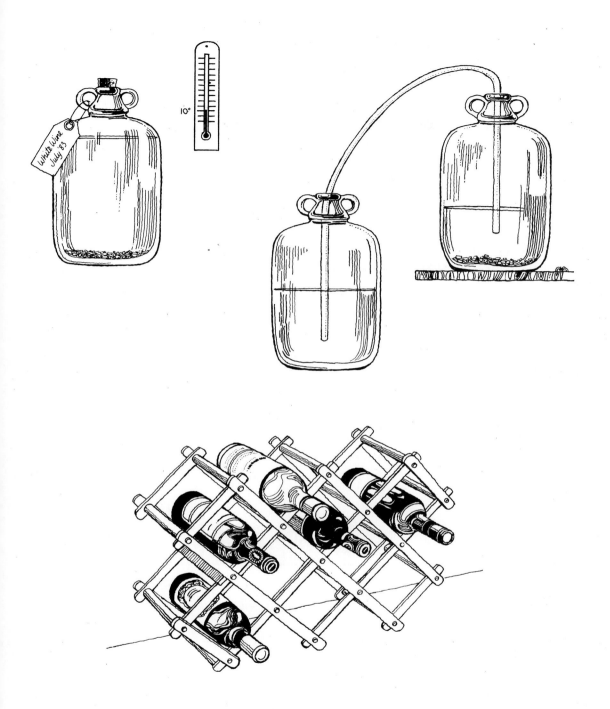

Writing

Write an account of how you make wine. Say what you do and what happens at each stage.

Unit 13   Summary of language

In this unit, you have learnt how to:
– describe the different stages of a process
– give instructions for making and operating things
– describe natural processes
– explain how things work

KEY POINTS

1 *Structures with 'When ...'*
   When you've turned the engine on, you should put the car in gear.
   When the butter melts, you should pour it into a bowl.

2 *Emphasising the right order*
   You should turn off the mains **before** you **change** the fuse.
   You shouldn't change the fuse **before/until** you've turned off the mains.

3 *The Passive*
   When a sample **has been written,** this **is typed** out neatly and **sent** to the
   publisher. This **is** then **read** by a publisher's reader.

4 *Causative verbs*
   The air pressure in the cylinder **prevents** the valve **from** opening.
   The air lock **allows** the carbon dioxide **to** escape.

5 *Vocabulary*
   utensils, equipment and ingredients
   'change of state' verbs
   parts of machines

Activities

LANGUAGE SCHOOL

Students A, B, C and D: You stopped going to English classes six months ago, and you now want to continue learning English. You decide to visit the four language schools in your town to see which you want to study at.
You are interested in:
a) the courses (levels, times, methods)
b) the fees
c) social activities

Think what questions you will ask, and what you will say about yourself.

Group 1: You work for the Anglo Language School.
Group 2: You work for the Britannia Language School.
Group 3: You work for the Continental Language School.
Group 4: You work for the Europa Language School.

In your groups, work out:
a) the kinds of courses you offer (levels, times, methods)
b) your fees
c) the social activities you offer
d) what questions you will ask prospective students

In turn, Students A, B, C and D visit each of the language schools, and have interviews.

COMPOSITION

Write 120–180 words on one of these topics:
1 You are studying at a language school. Write a letter to a friend telling him/her what it is like.
2 Write a prospectus for a language school.

Unit 14   Prediction

14.1   DEGREES OF PROBABILITY

Presentation and practice

Cable Television – Readers' views

Last week we reported plans to introduce American-style cable television to Britain – plans that would give the British viewer more than thirty TV channels to choose from, instead of the present four. Since then, hundreds of readers have sent us their views on the likely effects of cable TV. Here are some of them:

E.J. Jones, Cardiff: . . . Surely it's difficult enough to produce good programmes for only four channels. With 30 channels, the standard of programmes is bound to drop. And the Government is unlikely to be able to control all the programmes that go out – which means there could be a sharp increase in the amount of violence and sex on TV . . .

M. Saunders, Birmingham: . . . I was delighted to read about cable TV coming to Britain. With so many channels available, there are likely to be a lot more local programmes about topics of interest to the community . . .

Fiona Parker, Chepstow: . . . Cable TV is sure to bring even more American rubbish to our screens – more detectives, more soap operas, more dreadful quiz shows. Does anyone want to buy my TV? . . .

S. Mitchell, London: . . . Advertising companies are certain to welcome cable TV, but what about radio stations? Quite a lot of them may go out of business – after all, who can compete with 30 TV channels?

Martin Chapman, Exeter: . . . TV sales are likely to do well: there are bound to be some terrible arguments in one-TV families about which channel to watch. I know we'll have to get an extra set . . .

Mark each of the sentences below (1–9) with A, B, C, D, or E, according to the meanings of the readers' letters above.

A: This will certainly happen.
B: This will probably happen.
C: This might happen.
D: This probably won't happen.
E: This certainly won't happen.

1 The standard of programmes will drop.
2 The Government will be able to control cable TV programmes.
3 There will be an increase in the amount of sex and violence on TV.
4 There will be a lot more local programmes.
5 There will be more American programmes on British TV screens.
6 Advertising companies will welcome cable TV.
7 A lot of radio stations will go out of business.
8 TV sales will do well.
9 There will be more arguments about which channel to watch.

Practice

Change the sentences below, using **sure to, certain to, bound to, likely to** and **unlikely to**:

1 The price of bread will definitely go up within a few weeks.
2 There will probably be more fighting in the capital.
3 He probably won't arrive.
4 I expect there'll be lots of people at the meeting.
5 I doubt if the miners will go on strike.
6 There probably won't be much snow this winter.
7 There will definitely be a few tickets left.
8 I doubt if they'll move this summer.
9 I'm sure a new chairman will be appointed soon.
10 The Government probably won't make the wearing of seat belts compulsory.
11 In ten years' time everyone will have a digital watch.
12 By the end of the century, cars will probably be obsolete.

Work in groups. Cable TV is going to come to your area. Say what you think of the idea, and why.

14.2 PRECAUTIONS Practice

Examples A: Do you think I should take an umbrella?
　　　　　　B: Yes, you should – it's almost bound to rain.

　　　　　　A: Do you think I should take an umbrella?
　　　　　　B: There's no point – it's very unlikely to rain.

Work in pairs. Have similar conversations, beginning with these remarks:
1 Do you think I should reserve a table?
2 I suppose I could try to get a bank loan.
3 I was thinking of inviting her out to dinner.
4 Shall we take sandwiches?
5 Do you think I should apply?
6 Do you think I should buy some spare batteries?
7 Maybe I should get some malaria tablets before I go.

Capricorn

 Aquarius

This looks like a rather difficult week for you. You're likely to be criticised at work, and might find yourself in trouble at home, too. A letter will probably upset you. Beware of someone asking to borrow money – you're extremely unlikely to get it back. All this sounds rather depressing, but there's no point in worrying about it – things are certain to begin sorting themselves out towards the weekend. On a brighter note, you could receive a rather exciting invitation.

You may have minor problems at work, but don't be discouraged, as you are sure to overcome them in a day or two. Around the middle of the week you are likely to make new friends, and may begin an exciting new relationship. Your problems with money will slowly disappear, but be careful how you spend it as you may need it to help a friend. At the weekend there will probably be an opportunity to travel – you should take it, as it could lead to an important discovery.

Work in five groups. Choose two of the zodiac signs below, and write similar horoscopes for each.

Pisces

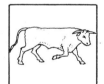

Taurus

Cancer

Virgo

Sagittarius

Aries

Gemini

Leo

Libra

Scorpio

14.4 CONDITIONAL PREDICTIONS   Presentation and practice

PART 1

You will hear four people making predictions about nuclear war. Listen, and match their predictions with the sentences below.

1 As long as both sides keep talking, there shouldn't be a nuclear war.
2 Unless both sides try harder to reach an understanding, there's likely to be a nuclear war.
3 Provided both sides maintain an adequate deterrent, there's not much danger of nuclear war.
4 If the arms race continues, there's almost bound to be a nuclear war.

PART 2

Now listen to these other predictions about nuclear war.
For each one:
a) Say whether the person is being optimistic or pessimistic.
b) Summarise what the person says in a single sentence, using **if, unless, as long as,** or **provided (that)**.

Work in groups.
Do you think there is likely to be a nuclear war in the near future?
Why/Why not?

14.5   IN YOUR LIFETIME

Free practice

You are going to conduct a survey of class opinion about the future.
Ask other people your two questions, and mark their answers in the table.
Answer questions other people ask you. Give reasons for your answers.

In your lifetime . . .
1 a) . . . will the world's supply of oil run out?
  b) . . . will we discover a major new source of energy?
2 a) . . . will China become the major world power?
  b) . . . will American influence in the world decline?
3 a) . . . will robots take over most manual work?
  b) . . . will the problem of unemployment be solved?
4 a) . . . will man colonise space?
  b) . . . will we discover life on other planets?
5 a) . . . will the world's population stop growing?
  b) . . . will starvation be eliminated?

Now report the results of your survey to the rest of the class.

	Yes	Likely	Maybe	Unlikely	No
1 a)					
b)					
2 a)					
b)					
3 a)					
b)					
4 a)					
b)					
5 a)					
b)					

Writing

Choose two of the questions above. Write a paragraph about each, saying what
you think will happen and why.

14.6 PREDICTING CONSEQUENCES

Presentation

The traffic in the centre of town is getting worse and worse, and the Council is planning to ban cars from the town centre during business hours.
Look at this letter to a local newspaper, and answer the questions.

Dear Sir,

If the traffic congestion gets any worse, there is likely to be a permanent traffic jam in the town centre during working hours, which will make it impossible for shops and businesses to operate efficiently.

The proposed scheme for banning cars from the centre is, however, unlikely to solve this problem. This ban will only cause more congestion in the suburbs, and in any case there are many people who genuinely need to take their cars to work.

A much better solution would be to double the number of train services into the centre, and to halve the fares. This would encourage people to stay off the roads, and would avoid the bad feeling that the present scheme seems likely to cause among the business community.

Yours faithfully,
MICHAEL B. TAYLOR,
25 Green Lane,
Burchester.

1 Why does the writer think:
   a) something should be done about traffic congestion?
   b) the proposed scheme will not work?
   c) his own solution is better?
2 Why does he use 'will' in paragraphs 1 and 2, and 'would' in paragraph 3?

Practice

Work in groups. Imagine the situations below exist in your town. Discuss:
a) what you think will happen if nothing is done
b) what is wrong with the proposed scheme
c) what you think should be done, and why

1 More and more cyclists are getting killed on main roads in the town. The Council is planning to restrict cyclists to the side streets.
2 A disused canal running through the town has had so much rubbish thrown into it that it is becoming a danger to health. The Council is planning to fill it in.
3 Vandalism is becoming more and more of a problem. The Council is planning to open a military-style detention centre for juvenile offenders.

Writing

Choose one of the topics you have discussed and write a letter to a local newspaper about it.

Reading

Read the following passage, which argues that men may live in space much sooner than we expect, and answer the questions.

The development of the Space Shuttle has dramatically reduced the cost of sending loads into space. The Shuttle takes off from Earth like a rocket, and lands again like an aircraft.
5 It can transport not only its own crew, but also passengers, and has a huge cargo-hold which is capable of carrying large satellites or a space laboratory.

Before the Space Shuttle was created, it was
10 necessary to plan trips into space several years in advance. However, for the rest of the century it should be possible to make space flights every week or so. Any scientist or engineer needing to travel into orbit will
15 simply take the next Shuttle flight, stay as long as necessary, and then return at his or her convenience.

It is difficult to imagine the immense opportunities created by the Shuttle. One of
20 the great advantages of having a reusable space vehicle is that it can take one load after another into orbit. Very large space stations could not be launched in their complete form directly from Earth, but they could be built
25 piece by piece in space. The Space Shuttle is likely to be used as a general 'workhorse' for the rest of this century, and the building of such stations in orbit should become commonplace.
30 Once these huge orbiting space stations are completed, they are likely to become the platforms from which hundreds of robot space ships could be launched cheaply and easily to explore the solar system and to start mining
35 operations on the Moon. The technology needed for this is already developed and available. And because of commercial and military pressures to develop space technology, it is likely that governments will
40 be increasingly willing to start extensive programmes of space engineering, exploration and research.

One future development could be the setting up of completely artificially constructed space
45 colonies. According to a growing number of experts, it is already technically feasible to

construct a pioneering space colony, powered by solar energy. This colony would be self-sufficient, and would also allow its inhabitants
50 to conduct further space engineering projects and build more colonies as they were needed. An American scientist, Dr Gerard O'Neill of Princeton University, has predicted that a space colony capable of supporting 10,000
55 humans could be set up well before the turn of the century. The materials for such a colony would have to be shipped up from Earth using the Space Shuttle. According to Dr O'Neill, further space colonies, which could house perhaps ten million people each, could be 60 constructed during the early part of the twenty-first century. These would not be made from earth materials, but would get their raw materials from the Moon.

(Adapted from *Future World*)

1 a) How is the Space Shuttle different from earlier space vehicles?
   b) What are the main advantages of the Space Shuttle?

2 What is its main use likely to be over the next 20 years?

3 Why couldn't a complete space station be launched directly from the earth?

4 What is the difference between a *space station* and a *space colony*, and what will each be used for?

5 Why do you think space colonies will eventually be constructed from moon rather than earth materials?

6 Why are governments likely to invest large amounts of money in space programmes?

7 Explain the following words and expressions as they are used in the passage:
   a) 'workhorse' (line 26)
   b) 'a pioneering space colony' (line 47)
   c) 'self-sufficient' (lines 48–9)
   d) 'raw materials' (lines 63–4)

Discussion

1 Do you think the developments predicted in the passage are really likely to happen? Why/Why not?
2 a) What benefits, if any, do you think might come from space programmes?
   b) What dangers, if any, do you think there might be?

Writing

Summarise in your own words the importance of the Space Shuttle and its probable uses in the future. Write 80–100 words.

Work in groups. Discuss how you think a space colony might work, and what
you think life would be like on it.
Talk about:

gravity	leisure
oxygen	travel
food and water	isolation
the environment	children

Unit 14   Summary of language

In this unit, you have learnt how to:
– predict future actions and events
– say how likely things are to happen
– make conditional predictions
– predict consequences of future actions and imagine alternatives

KEY POINTS

1 *Infinitive structures expressing probability*
   Prices are **bound to** rise again soon.
   There are **certain to** be protests about the new law.
   You are **likely to** have problems at work this month.
   There is **unlikely to** be much support for the campaign.

2 *'Conditional' predictions*

   | **If** **As long as** **Provided (that)** | they can get reinforcements they should win. |
   | **Unless** they can **If** they can't | get reinforcements, they are unlikely to win. |

3 *Predicting consequences and imagining alternatives*
   The Council is planning to pull down old houses in the city centre and build
   offices instead. If they do this more people **will** become homeless, and it **is**
   likely to spoil the atmosphere of the town. It **would** be better to improve the
   houses and let people continue to live in them. This **would** cost less and
   would help the town to keep its character.

Activities

STORY-TELLING

Work in pairs. You are either Pair A or Pair B.

Pair A: Look at pictures 1–8 of the picture story by the French cartoonist Sempé, and decide what it is about. Practise telling the story.

Pair B: Look at pictures 9–14 of the picture story by the French cartoonist Sempé, and decide what it is about.
Practise telling the story.

Now form new pairs (one A and one B) and tell each other your part of the story (starting with A).

1 2

3 4

5

6

7

8

⫸

9

10

11

COMPOSITION

Write the story told by the pictures in 120–180 words.

Unit 15   News

15.1   THE NEWS   Presentation and practice

You will hear part of a radio broadcast.
Listen to the tape once. Say briefly what each news item is about.
Listen to each news item again, and make brief notes in answer to the questions below.

Item 1:   What has happened?
    When, where and how did it happen?
    What has been happening since then?
    What has happened since then?

Item 2:   What has been happening at 10 Downing St?
    What has been achieved?

Item 3:   What has the Government failed to do?
    What has the union done?
    What two things happened earlier this afternoon?

Item 4:   What has been happening in southern France?
    What hasn't happened?
    What four things have happened?

Item 5:   What has been happening in Manchester?
    What does the news item say about:
    a) Mrs Jane Simpkins?
    b) articles found at the murder scene?
    c) the detective-superintendent in charge of the case?
    d) house-to-house inquiries?

Work in groups. From your notes, reconstruct each news item.

15.2   HEADLINE NEWS

Practice

Work in groups. Look at the six headlines, and make up the story that each
refers to. Consider:
– what has happened
– the details of what happened

– what has/hasn't happened since
– what has been happening
– what is going to happen

Airport collision: 20 killed

Peace talks break down

Roman treasure discovered in field

Actor arrested in night club brawl

Residents evacuated after earthquake

Search for missing yacht 'Melissa' continues

Writing

Choose two of the headlines, and write the story of each.

Imagine that someone tells you this piece of news.
What questions might you ask?

'Have you heard? Apparently there's been a robbery in the High Street.'

Work in groups.

1 Choose one of the local pieces of news below.

   Imagine what the whole story is, so that you can answer any questions you
   might be asked about it.
   a) There's been a demonstration in town.
   b) A tiger's been seen on the loose.
   c) The . . . Hotel has been burnt down.
   d) . . . has been arrested.
   e) . . . has got engaged.

2 Talk to other people in the class. Announce your piece of news, and answer
   any questions they ask you about it.

   Other people will tell you their news. Ask them for details, *unless* you have
   already heard all about it from somebody else.

15.4 YOUR OWN NEWS   Free practice

Work in groups. Tell each other about a real piece of news,
either of local interest
or   about yourself and people that you know

15.5 HEARSAY

Presentation

They say he's terribly stingy.
He's **supposed to be** terribly stingy.

Apparently he's living in Paris.
He's **supposed to be living** in Paris.

I hear he had a heart attack two years ago.
He's **supposed to have had** a heart attack two years ago.

In the same way, change the following remarks using **supposed to**:
1   Apparently elephants have very long memories.
2   People say it's unlucky to walk under a ladder.
3   They say there's a monster in Loch Ness.
4   Apparently Marilyn Monroe was an insomniac.
5   I'm told that garlic stops you catching a cold.
6   Apparently Venice is slowly sinking into the sea.
7   I'm told that he was a lorry driver at one time.
8   They say that Methuselah lived for more than 300 years.
9   I've heard that student grants are going up next year.
10 People say she was born on board a ship.
11 They say the universe is expanding all the time.

Practice

Answer these questions, making it clear that your answers are based on hearsay, and not on personal knowledge or experience. Use **supposed to, apparently, I hear, I'm told, people/they say.**

1   Do you know if Alsatians make good pets?
2   What does it feel like to be hypnotised?
3   I'm thinking of going to see (*name of film*). Do you know what it's like?
4   I wonder what's happening in (*name of country in the news*)?
5   What do you think (*famous person*) is like as a person?
6   I wonder what it's like to actually live in Hollywood?
7   Do you know anything about life in Ancient Greece?

15.6 PASSIVE REPORTING VERBS

Presentation and practice

A reporter has collected information from several sources about a civil war he is covering. Most of the people he has talked to think that the capital is still in the hands of rebel troops. In his report, he could say:

'**It is thought that** the capital is still in the hands of rebel troops.'
or 'The capital **is thought to be** still in the hands of rebel troops.'

Here are some more pieces of information that he has found out. Report them in the same way.
1 Some people report that the American Government is worried about the situation.
2 Sources estimate that more than 100 people have died in the past two days.
3 Everyone knows that the rebels' weapons came across the border by road.
4 A lot of people believe that the President is about to resign.
5 People say that the rebels are winning.
6 Some sources allege that both sides have tortured prisoners.

Practice

Imagine you are the reporter. Your editor has cabled you for information about:
1 ordinary people in the capital and in the countryside
2 food supplies
3 hospitals
4 support for each side
5 the rebel leader

15.7 TODAY'S NEWS   Free practice

Work in groups. Your teacher will give you the first sentence of an item of today's news.
1 Discuss what the complete news story is.
2 Write the story for inclusion in a radio news broadcast.

Reading

The three passages below all appeared in British newspapers in May 1981.

Charles tapes — the storm grows

THE QUEEN was said last night to be 'appalled' at claims that some of Prince Charles' personal phone calls home from Australia had been tapped and recorded.

The publishers of a West German magazine aimed at middle-aged housewives said that they might publish the transcripts of the royal conversations on Monday.

There are said to be tapes of four phone conversations between the Prince and Lady Diana, and one between him and the Queen in which he is alleged to have been rude about Australians in general and their Prime Minister Malcolm Fraser in particular.

The tapes were offered to the Germans by a British journalist, Mr Simon Regan, who was in Australia to do research for a book. While he was there, he came into contact with an anti-British Australian republican group, who brought the recordings to his hotel in Sydney.

'The tapes fell into my lap' said Mr Regan. 'I heard four of the five tapes and I am convinced they are genuine because they contained aspects of Prince Charles' and Lady Diana's life which no-one else could have known about.'

1 In what two ways might the tapes be embarrassing to the Royal Family?
2 Why do you think:
   a) the republican group tapped the conversations?
   b) they were given to Mr Regan?
3 What kind of articles would you expect in general to find in the West German magazine?
4 a) What did Mr Regan mean by 'The tapes fell into my lap'?
   b) What do you think of his reason for believing the tapes?

Queen's 'distaste' at press payments

THE QUEEN has joined the controversy over 'chequebook journalism' in the case of the Yorkshire Ripper, who is on trial accused of the murder of 13 women. A letter from the Queen's deputy private secretary said she shared the 'distaste of all right-minded people'.

The letter was sent to Mrs Doreen Hill, the mother of the Ripper's last victim, who had written to the Queen about reports that large payments were to be made to the family of the killer, Peter Sutcliffe.

Mrs Hill claims that newspapers have offered a total of around £150,000 to Sutcliffe's friends and relatives. Her solicitor said yesterday: 'She is outraged that the Press can do this. The *Daily Mail* admitted to us last Friday that they were going to pay John Sutcliffe, the father of the accused, £10,000 for his story after the trial.'

Moves to outlaw chequebook journalism are being considered by the Government.

1 What do you think 'chequebook journalism' is?
2 Why was Mrs Hill 'outraged', and why did the Queen send her a letter?
3 Why might the incident be considered 'distasteful'?
4 Say in your own words what the Government is doing.

Manufacturing a news story

MONDAY 4 MAY. It's 10.35 a.m. and there are 389 media people in Belfast, most, it would seem, in the Europa Hotel, and all are looking for a war.

For the first time in 12 years of covering the world's conflicts and especially the troubles in Northern Ireland, I have been forced to question seriously the objectivity of some of my colleagues.

There have been reports of photographers paying youths to throw rocks and bottles at passing army vehicles. One US TV crew is said to have such an incident filmed.

In the Lower Falls a TV crew was seen by police inciting rioters to do damage on a building site, and in another incident a TV crew was seen directing rioters to create action which was then filmed.

The very presence of photographers and TV crews on street

above: Blazing wheelbarrows

corners in Belfast seems to induce youths to throw things at passing security vehicles.

Last weekend I was approached by youths in the Falls Road asking what I wanted them to do. When I said I didn't want them to do anything, I was informed that some foreign journalists always paid them. This was substantiated by colleagues, many of whom received similar approaches.

---

1 In what ways, according to the writer, are photographers and TV crews adding to the violence in Northern Ireland?
2 What evidence does he have of this?
3 Why do you think some foreign journalists behaved in this way?
4 Why does the writer find this shocking?

Discussion

1 a) In what ways are the three examples of 'chequebook journalism' similar?
   b) In what ways are they different?
2 Do you approve or disapprove of what happened in each case? Why?
3 What controls, if any, do you think there should be on the freedom of the Press?

Writing

Write a letter (100–150 words) to a newspaper, giving your reaction to one or more of the news items you have read.

Unit 15   Summary of language

In this unit, you have learnt how to:
– announce news
– give details of news
– report things you have heard from other people

KEY POINTS

1 *Present Perfect and Past tenses*
   Shops and offices **have been** damaged by a serious fire in the town centre,
   which start**ed** late last night and rag**ed** for five hours until firemen **brought** it
   under control early this morning. Police **have** closed the street to traffic, and
   experts **have been** trying to find out how the fire start**ed**.

2 *'Supposed to'*
   Apparently the Welsh mountains are very beautiful.
   The Welsh mountains **are supposed to be** very beautiful.

   They say he's left the country.
   He's **supposed to have** left the country.

3 *Other reporting verbs*
   Many people **think that** the Vikings sailed to Canada.
   It is thought that the Vikings sailed to Canada.
   The Vikings **are thought to have** sailed to Canada.

   According to reports, the spacecraft is approaching Saturn.
   It is reported that the spacecraft is approaching Saturn.
   The spacecraft **is reported to be** approaching Saturn.

Activities

THE FUTURE OF SANTA CLARA

The island of Santa Clara depends entirely on fishing, and is very poor. The Government of Santa Clara is considering whether to develop tourism on the island to increase the prosperity of the inhabitants.
A television discussion is planned to debate the issue.

Student A: You believe that tourism should be developed. Use the diagram to help you develop your arguments.

Student B: You think it would be wrong to develop tourism. Use the diagram to help you develop your arguments.

Student C: You are the interviewer in charge of the discussion. Use the diagram to decide what questions you will ask.

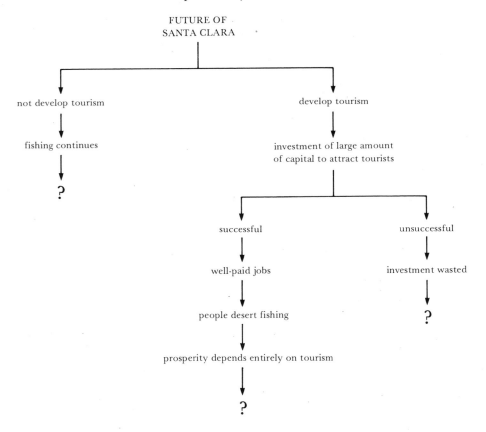

Now form new groups (one A, one B and one C) and conduct the discussion.

COMPOSITION

Write a newspaper article (120–180 words) about the future of Santa Clara.
State the arguments for and against developing tourism and come to a
conclusion.

SITUATIONS

1 You've just had some very good news. Tell someone about it.
2 You're teaching a friend to drive. Remind him/her what order to do things in,
   before starting off.
3 A child asks you 'Why does the kitchen window get all wet when you're
   cooking?' Explain.
4 You've heard some gossip about someone. Pass it on to a friend.
5 Someone asks you 'Do you think we'll ever be able to control the weather?'.
   Express your opinion.
6 You want someone to take a photo of you, but he/she doesn't know how to
   use your camera. Tell him.
7 A friend who is going away to college is worried in case he/she can't manage
   away from home. Reassure him/her.

Unit 16 Revision

16.1 DESCRIBING PEOPLE

Look at the four people in the photographs.
1 Describe their physical appearance.
2 How old do you think they are? What nationalities are they?
3 Imagine that you know one of them. Give a complete description of the
person, including the following:
  a) job and daily routine
  b) life-style and habits
  c) leisure activities, skills, likes and dislikes
  d) character and attitudes
  e) a short account of his/her past life

Write a full description of the person you have chosen.

16.2 TAKING AND DIRECTING ACTION

Have short conversations based on these situations.
1 A and B aren't sure what to do at the weekend. They discuss the various possibilities and come to a decision.
2 A is thinking of hitchhiking across the country. B is an experienced hitchhiker, and gives him some advice, and tells him what precautions to take, and why.
3 A, a student, wants to borrow a cassette recorder from school. B, a teacher, isn't very happy about the idea.
4 A has just started living in a students' hostel. She asks B, another resident, what she can do and what she can't do.
5 A is a tourist, who just wants to wander round on her own. B is a local, who offers to help her in various ways.
6 A wants to cook a particular dish, but doesn't know how to do it. B gives him some instructions.

Discuss the two topics below. In each case:
1 Talk about:
   a) what it used to be like / what used to happen
   b) how it has and hasn't changed
   c) what it is like now / what happens now
2 Say whether things have improved or got worse, and in what ways.

Talk about:
1 Education 50 years ago and education now.
2 The position of women 50 years ago and now.

Write about 150 words on one of the topics.

16.4 DESCRIBING PLACES

Describe the town you are living in. Include information about:
1 geographical location
2 general information: size, population, main occupations, etc
3 amenities:
   a) services
   b) sports and leisure
   c) culture and entertainment
4 any important buildings and say how to get to them from where you are now

Write a full description of the town.

16.5 RECENT ACTIONS AND ACTIVITIES

You've just met a friend whom you haven't seen for some time. Tell him/her:

1 what you've been doing recently
2 what you've done recently
3 things that have changed in your life
4 things that are the same as before
5 what you're doing at the moment

Write the information in a letter.

16.6 DESCRIBING A SCENE

Look at the picture above.
1 What is happening?
2 What do you think has happened?
3 What else is there in the picture?

Imagine that you saw this scene. Describe what you saw, and what happened next.

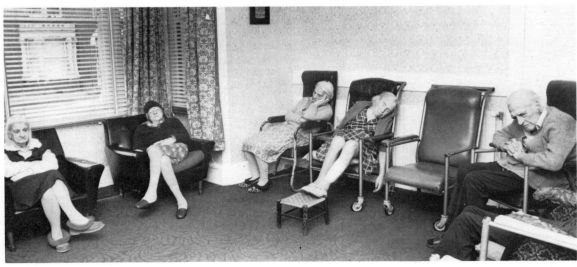

Choose one of the pictures above and:
1 Say what major problem or problems it suggests to you.
2 Explain in detail what these problems are, and how they arose.
3 Say what you think *should* be done about them, and why.
4 Say what you think *will* happen.

Write about 150 words on the topic you have discussed.

16.8 NARRATION CHOICES

1 Tell a joke you have heard.
2 Report a conversation you heard or took part in recently.
3 Retell one of the stories that you told, heard, read or wrote during this
  course.

Write one of the jokes, reports or stories that you told.

16.9 QUESTIONS

This is a Lateral Thinking game. Look at the information below, and try to work out the whole story, so that the events make sense. You can ask any questions that can be answered with 'Yes' or 'No'.

A man goes into a building. He comes out again holding a box. He opens the box, looks inside, closes it again, throws it away, and walks down the street smiling.

When you have solved the problem, write the whole story in the past.

16.10 SPEECHES

Prepare a two-minute talk on one of the topics below:

being unemployed	wishes
dishwashers	policemen
working as a tourist guide	teaching
mousetraps	wine
package holidays	cable TV
outer space	

Write the speech which you made.

MURDERER'S CONFESSION (6.8)

It was lunchtime the next day when Lestrade returned to Sherlock Holmes' rooms in 221B, Baker Street.

'Well, you were right again, Holmes,' he sighed, and handed over a piece of paper which contained a confession of murder.

Holmes took the paper and began to read.

'My step-mother married my father for his money. I tried to warn him, but he would take no notice of me. He trusts her absolutely.

'As soon as she heard about my engagement to Anna, she tried to stop the wedding, as she wanted all of my father's fortune for herself. She knew about Anna's affair with Grimes because she is herself having an affair with him, and he must have told her about it.

'She threatened to tell my father about the affair if we did not call off the wedding. He would certainly have cut me out of his will altogether if he had known. He hates any kind of scandal. But Anna and I were deeply in love, and were determined that my step-mother should not spoil our happiness.

'I begged my step-mother not to tell my father – I told her there was enough money for both of us – but she wouldn't listen. Then I went to Grimes: perhaps he could persuade my step-mother to keep quiet. But he only laughed in my face – he planned to get a share of my father's money after my step-mother had inherited it. I lost my temper. We had a fight and my glasses were broken. I'm rather short-sighted.

'After that I decided the only way to solve the problem was to kill my step-mother, and to make it look like suicide. I copied her handwriting and wrote a suicide note. I didn't tell Anna about my plan – though now I wish I had.

'Yesterday morning, I went to my step-mother's dressing room carrying a gun and the suicide note. I opened the door quietly and looked inside. I couldn't see very well without my glasses, but I saw a woman with long, dark hair standing with her back to me. I crept up behind her, shot her in the head, dropped the suicide note and put the gun in her hand. As I did this, I recognised the woman's face, and realised that I had killed Anna. She must have been waiting to speak to my step-mother – to beg her not to tell my father about her affair with Grimes.

'What could I do? I could hear my step-mother moving in her bathroom, which was next door, so I ran off as quickly as I could. Then she found the body and called the police.'

Listening texts

1.3 HAVE YOU EVER . . .?

A: Do you know at the weekend, we went out and had a meal in a Japanese restaurant. And it was absolutely amazing, I mean they gave us all this raw fish and stuff, and it was terribly neat and tidy, beautifully presented and quite different from anything I'd expected. Have you ever eaten Japanese food?

B: Yes, I have but only once. A friend took me to a Japanese restaurant to celebrate his birthday and we had sukiyaki or something – I don't know. I didn't like it at all to be honest.

A: Do you know, someone shouted at me in the street this afternoon. I was walking along you know just minding my own business when this man came up and started shouting at me, started calling me names. I couldn't believe it. Have you ever been shouted at in the street like that?

B: No, I haven't, not like that. Er, well I have been shouted at but it was by a policeman. I mean it was a bit different. You see, I was driving and I drove straight through a red light.

A: Oh dear, someone stole my bike last night. I'm furious because it was entirely my own fault. I went to a party and I just left it outside the house where the party was without a padlock on. Not surprisingly when I came out it was gone. Have you ever had your bike stolen?

B: Yes, I have. Mine was stolen about a month ago as a matter of fact. I did exactly the same thing as you – I left it in the street without the padlock on. Luckily I got it back.

2.5 DESCRIBING PEOPLE

The man has got straight, dark hair – it's fairly short – he's got a parting, .. er ... he's slightly bald – with a receding hairline. He's got sideburns on each side of his face. He's got a square face, with quite a few wrinkles. His nose is slightly crooked; he's got a cleft chin.

The woman has shoulder-length wavy blond hair. She's got quite a long face, with a pointed chin, and her nose is long and pointed, too. She's got thin lips, and freckles, and she's got a dimple in one cheek.

4.1 EXPRESSING ATTITUDES

Presenter: Thank you. So that's the question. Angela, perhaps you'd like to start . . .

Angela: Well . . . er . . . on the whole I find television commercials extremely annoying. I mean, you're watching a film on television perhaps, and suddenly you're interrupted by these stupid commercials with a silly format which have nothing to do with the film you're watching, and they completely destroy your concentration. That really irritates me.

Presenter: Edward.

Edward: Well I must say I agree with Angela. I get particularly upset when I see these hordes of well-known people appearing in commercials, seemingly just to make a lot of money and pretending to believe in the product they're advertising. It upsets me. And that's what depresses me more than anything else, it's . . . ordinary members of the public actually believing what these commercials tell them. I think it's very sad.

Presenter: Sheila, do commercials have that sort of effect on you?

Sheila: Well, it's obvious that Edward's offended because he hasn't been asked to appear in a commercial. I couldn't disagree more actually. You see, it's true that not all commercials are good but a lot of them are very interesting and very amusing and some of them are even more interesting than the programmes. And of course there is a very important point about commercials whether you like them or whether you agree with them, whether you believe in them or not – is that the thing is, they do pay for the programmes. And without the commercials we wouldn't have the programmes at all, so I think that Angela and Edward are both being terribly one-sided and in fact their attitude really astonishes me.

Presenter: Well before we pass on to the next . . .

4.5 THE WAY

Presenter: . . . we asked various people what they thought about the police . . .

A: Well, what I like about them is the way they're so helpful. You know – the way they can always find time to help when you need directions, if you're lost or something.

B: I resent the way the police react quite differently to different groups of people – I mean, for example, their reaction to young people and students, youths, they may have long hair, very short hair, skin heads – is quite different from people who are, you know, sort of middle-aged, they have well-spoken middle-class voices. It's quite wrong.

C: The thing that impresses me about them is the way they manage to keep control of crowds and things so effectively . . . I mean we've been to some wonderful functions here in London and it's tremendous . . . I mean they don't carry guns or anything like that. They're a great bunch of guys.

D: What I like most about them is the way they're so frightfully polite. I mean, I find that if ever I ask them a question, they call me 'Madam' and they're just generally polite. I do like them.

E: I get very annoyed by the way they ask you so many questions. They seem so slow and stupid sometimes which really gets on my nerves.

5.1 HOW LONG?

Dialogue A

A: Hullo, Fred. Did you do anything exciting last night?

B: No, I just played cards with some friends.

A: You look pretty worn out. How long did you play for?

B: Oh, we played for about five hours. What about you?

A: Me? Oh I had to drive my sister to Heathrow. She was catching a plane to Canada.

B: How long did that take you?

A: It wasn't too bad. I got there and back by 11.30.

Dialogue B

A: Where were you last night?

B: I was baby-sitting for Wendy and Paul, actually.

A: Really? You must have been late, because I phoned you at midnight. How long did you have to baby-sit for?

B: Oh, I was there until about one in the morning.

A: That late? I hope they gave you a lift home.

B: Not a chance. I walked.

A: You're joking – it must be about five miles to your place from Wendy's. How long did it take you to walk all that way?

B: Not all that long, actually. I got home in less than an hour. I'm a fast walker.

5.4 HOW LONG DOES IT TAKE?

A: How long does it take to drive across London?

B: Well, that depends on the traffic. If the roads aren't too busy, you can do it in about an hour. But if you go during the rush hour, then of course it can take much longer.

C: Yes, of course it also depends on how well you know the roads. If you don't know the best routes, it can take you hours to get through, because you'll get stuck in one-way systems and end up miles away from where you want to go to. If I were you I'd have a good look at a street map before you set out . . .

6.4 KINDS OF STATEMENT

A: Two months ago, Mr Jim Lock, of Kimberley Road, Croydon, received a visit from a salesman representing Bargain Electrics Ltd, who persuaded him to buy an electric drill for £60. He told Mr Lock that if he sent a £15 deposit, they would send him the drill on a two-week home trial. If, after that time, he didn't want to keep the drill, he should send it back and his deposit would be refunded. The salesman assured Mr Lock that he was under no obligation to buy the drill if he didn't like it.

B: Mr Lock sent his deposit and received the drill a few days later. But when he tried it out he found it didn't work, and the same afternoon his wife saw exactly the same drill in a local shop for only £50.

A: So he sent the drill back to Bargain Electrics with a letter. In the letter he explained that he didn't want the drill because it didn't work and pointed out that the same drill could be bought locally for £10 less.

B: Instead of getting his deposit back, as he expected, Mr Lock got a letter from Bargain Electrics in which they claimed that he had broken the drill by using it wrongly, and that he still owed them £45.

A: So Mr Lock wrote back to them. He strongly denied that he had broken the drill, and asked them again to return his £15.

B: A few days later he got a letter from the Managing Director, who insisted that the drill had reached Mr Lock in perfect condition, and warned him that if he did not pay the balance within seven days, the company would have to take legal action.

A: At this point, Mr Lock contacted us, and we phoned Bargain Electrics. We spoke to the Sales Manager, who at first accused us of interfering in a private matter, but eventually agreed to have the drill inspected.

B: The next morning we had a very polite phone call from the Managing Director himself, who admitted that Mr Lock had been right all along, and that the drill had been wrongly assembled in the factory.

A: And we're pleased to say that the very next day Mr Lock received his £15 deposit – and a new drill. He assures us that the new drill works perfectly.

Dialogue 1

A: Poor old George. Fancy having an awful job like that. They must pay him well.
B: Oh, I don't know. He can't earn much – look at that old car he drives.
A: That doesn't prove anything – he might enjoy driving an old car.
B: Maybe, but he can't enjoy wearing that dreadful old suit of his.
A: Mm, that's true. Well, in that case, why doesn't he resign?

Dialogue 2

A: Is Hilda here?
B: No, it's her lunch hour. Try the canteen – she may be having a snack with Jimmy.
A: No, she isn't. I've just come from there.
B: Hm. She must have gone out to a restaurant, then.
A: Well she can't have gone far. Her coat's still here.
B: Ah, in that case she might be having a curry at the Taj Mahal – it's only round the corner.

Dialogue 3

A: It's obvious what happened. He must have been sitting in bed smoking the pipe. Then he fell asleep and dropped the pipe, which set fire to the bedclothes, and he was suffocated by the smoke.
B: Ah but there are two things you don't know. First he can't have been smoking the pipe – he gave up smoking at least a year ago . . .
A: He might have started again!
B: Second, when his lungs were examined, there was no trace of smoke in them. So he must have stopped breathing *before* the fire started . . .

7.6   EXPLANATIONS

About seven out of ten people released from prison end up in prison again sooner or later. A lot of people think this simply indicates that once a person becomes a criminal he will probably remain a criminal. But of course it doesn't necessarily mean that at all. On the contrary, it could equally suggest that being in prison actually makes people more likely to commit crimes. After all, prisons are full of criminals, and this means that someone going to prison for the first time is going to meet a lot more criminals than he's met before. So he'll probably learn a lot about crime during his stay there. The fact that so many people get re-arrested also suggests that prisons aren't doing enough to train people for jobs they can do when they get out. If they were given this training, ex-prisoners wouldn't need to turn to crime again to make a living.

8.1   GOOD AND BAD EFFECTS

The inhabitants of Tango, a small island in the South Pacific, discovered a plant which contained a powerful drug. This drug made it more difficult for them to think rationally – it stopped them worrying about the future, and enabled them to forget all their problems. At the same time, it made it much easier for them to relax and enjoy themselves: so much so, indeed, that the whole population of the island stopped working and spent all their time singing and dancing and looking at the sea. Unfortunately this had a very bad effect on the country's economy, and people began to run short of food. This, however didn't discourage the people from taking the drug. The Prime Minister made speeches on the TV warning them about the drug, but nobody took any notice, and before long the economy was in ruins. This forced the Government to make the drug illegal. But that only made the situation worse. The law couldn't prevent the people from taking the drug, which grew wild all over the island; on the contrary, the fact that the drug was illegal merely encouraged people to take it. Eventually, the Government found a better solution: they exported the drug to other countries. This saved the islanders from having to work more than one day a week, and allowed them to spend the rest of their time sitting in the sun without a care in the world.

9.6 YOU'VE GOT IT ALL WRONG 🔲

A: Richard bought a cassette recorder in Hong Kong, didn't he?
B: No, it wasn't Richard who bought it, it was Alan.
C: Anyway, it wasn't a cassette recorder that he bought, it was a radio.
D: Anyway, it wasn't in Hong Kong that he bought it, it was in Singapore.
A: I see – so Alan bought a radio in Singapore then. Is that right?

10.3 FANTASIES 🔲

A: If I had just one day I would go back to New York. I'd go up the Empire State Building, and I would take the ferry to Coney Island, and I would go on the funfair, and I would have a hot-dog and French fries and a very large glass of Coca Cola; and finally I think I would probably go to a show, and get a very expensive ticket and get the best seat in the house – and then I would fly home.
B: Well, if I could go anywhere in the world, I think I'd, I'd go to to Tibet and I'd go to Lhasa and I'd sit in a tea-house in Lhasa and I'd just watch people for an hour and then I'd get on a bus, I mean if they have buses in Tibet, and I'd travel through as much of Tibet as I could in one day.
C: If I could spend a day doing anything I wanted to, I'd like to go to London. I'd like to go to London and I'd like to buy some wonderful expensive clothes in a really . . . high-class shop and then, in the evening, I'd like to go out to one of these really expensive candle-lit restaurants and then afterwards I'd stay at a really nice hotel, you know nothing too . . . classy like the Savoy but really nice, really expensive.

12.5 WHAT IS IT? 🔲

A: Right, um, it's made of pottery.
B: Pottery, mm. Is this object bigger or smaller than a refrigerator?
A: Oh, much smaller.
B: I see. How big is it compared to a flower pot?
A: Um – it's a bit smaller than a flower pot.
C: Does it have a similar shape to a packet of cigarettes?
A: No, it doesn't.
C: What about a flower pot? Is it the same shape as a flower pot?
A: Yes, it's about the same shape as a flower pot.

B: Would I use it more often than I'd use a flower pot?
A: Oh yes, much more often.
B: More often than a packet of cigarettes?
A: Well that depends on how much you smoke.
C: Might I use it at the same time as I use a packet of cigarettes?
A: You might do, yes.
C: Is it a coffee cup?
A: Yes, it is.

13.3 GIVING INSTRUCTIONS

A: How do you make Turkish coffee? What is it you have to do exactly?
B: Well, say you want to make four cups of coffee. O.K.? You put four cups of cold
water, and four level teaspoons of sugar in the coffee pot. Then you light the gas,
and put the coffee on the stove. Now when the water boils, you take the coffee pot
off the stove and pour a bit of the water into one of the cups. Then you put the four
heaped teaspoons of coffee in the coffee pot, and stir it. Now it's very important not
to put the coffee in before you've poured some water off, or else it'll overflow and
make a terrible mess. So anyway, you put the pot back on the stove and let the
coffee come back to the boil very slowly. When it starts to boil, the coffee will rise
slowly up to the top of the pot, and when it reaches the top, you take it off the stove.
O.K.? Before you pour the coffee out, you should pour back the water that you
poured off earlier – this helps to make the grounds settle. See? O.K.?
A: Yes, thanks very much.

14.4 CONDITIONAL PREDICTIONS

Part 1

Yes I think as things are at the moment we're in quite a lot of danger. Well, the trouble
is um the two sides really need to talk a lot more, well see the other side's point of view,
otherwise it does seem rather hopeless.

I think um the balance of power is keeping us out of any real danger of war, I mean as
things are at the moment neither side would really dare to start a war because of the
consequences.

Well I think it's really a question of keeping dialogue going – you know the SALT talks
– things like that. I think if that ever stopped altogether then well, we'd really have
something to worry about.

I don't see any way out really, I mean it doesn't matter how much they talk about a
deterrent, all the time they're making new weapons and eventually there are going to be
so many weapons around that someone's going to start using them, it's inevitable.

Part 2

I think things are fairly well under control really – the only real danger is if someone
starts a war accidentally.

The only thing I worry about is someone pressing the button before anyone can stop him – you know, some madman – otherwise I think we'll survive O.K.

The trouble is I think more and more countries are getting nuclear weapons and that's getting really dangerous. We've really got to stop nuclear weapons spreading.

Well obviously neither of the superpowers wants to start a war. The only danger is if they both get drawn into a crisis on opposite sides.

Well, I really think the United Nations helps a lot because it provides a place where people can talk. I think with the UN there countries would always stop short of an actual nuclear war.

15.1 THE NEWS

The time is 4 o'clock. Here is the news summary.

There has been a serious accident on the M6 motorway in Lancashire, in which at least six people have lost their lives. It happened early this morning near Preston when a coach carrying 45 passengers collided with a heavy lorry. Rescue operations have been going on throughout the day, and a section of the motorway has been closed to traffic.

Important talks have been taking place at 10 Downing Street today between the Prime Minister and Trade Union leaders. They have agreed to work together to find ways of combating inflation and reducing the present level of unemployment in British industry.

Meanwhile, the Government has failed to avert a national bus strike, and the bus drivers' union has announced that no buses will run from next Monday. The decision to go ahead with the strike was announced by a union spokesman at the end of a meeting earlier this afternoon during which Government representatives failed to persuade the union and the employers to agree on a new wage plan.

The forest fire in southern France: firemen from six different towns have been fighting all day to prevent the fire from spreading further. Latest reports say that the blaze has still not been brought under control, and that an estimated three million pounds' worth of damage has already been caused. Four people have died in the fire so far, and 20 more have been taken to hospital with burns and other injuries. The French Government has asked all tourists to avoid the area.

Police in Manchester have been continuing their search for the murderer of 71-year-old Mrs Jane Simpkins, who was found beaten to death in the kitchen of her home two days ago. Articles found at the murder scene have been taken away for examination by police experts, and the detective-superintendent in charge of the case has appealed for information from members of the public. This morning detectives began making house-to-house inquiries in the immediate neighbourhood.

Drills

Drill 1   Asking about experiences

I went to the Caribbean last summer.
Have you ever been to the Caribbean?

The police stopped me in the street yesterday.
Have you ever been stopped in the street by the police?

Someone picked my pocket on Tuesday.
Have you ever had your pocket picked?

Drill 2   Familiarity and unfamiliarity

They drive on the right.
She's not used to driving on the right.

And they stare at her.
She's not used to being stared at.

There's not much water, so she can't have a bath every day.
She's used to having a bath every day.

Drill 3   Sense impressions

Look at that man. Is he going to jump into the water?
He looks as if he's going to jump into the water.

Can I try some? Mm. Camembert, isn't it?
It tastes like Camembert.

What's wrong with your voice? Have you got a cold?
You sound as if you've got a cold.

Drill 4   Seem

He's changed somehow.
He seems to have changed somehow.

It's as if he's dreaming all the time.
He seems to be dreaming all the time.

As far as I can tell, he doesn't recognise me any more.
He doesn't seem to recognise me any more.

Drill 5   Previous events

Brian forgot to set his alarm, so he woke up late.
Brian woke up late because he had forgotten to set his alarm.

He woke up late so he left the house in a hurry.
He left the house in a hurry because he had woken up late.

Drill 6   Previous activities

Well, there were some cards on the table.
Ah, so they'd been playing cards, had they?

And most of my chocolates were missing.
Ah, so they'd been eating your chocolates, had they?

LAB SESSION 2 (UNITS 4–6)

Drill 1   Attitudes

I like men with long beards. They impress me.
I see. So you find men with long beards impressive.

I don't like shy men. They irritate me.
I see. So you find shy men irritating.

Drill 2   Strong feelings

Susan doesn't pay back her debts. She makes me angry.
If there's one thing that makes me angry it's people who don't pay back their debts.

Tom has bad breath. I can't stand him.
If there's one thing I can't stand, it's people who have bad breath.

Drill 3   Take and spend

I did the washing in twenty minutes.
It took me twenty minutes to do the washing.

He watched television the whole evening.
He spent the whole evening watching television.

Drill 4   How long?

I once lived in Russia, you know.
How long did you live in Russia?

They're coming to stay next week.
How long are they staying?

I think he's ill.
How long has he been ill?

Drill 5   Reported speech

You were born abroad.
She told me that I had been born abroad.

Your lucky number is seven.
She told me that my lucky number was seven.

Drill 6   Reporting verbs

Difficult times lie ahead. (warn)
He warned us that difficult times lay ahead.

I know – I know – we haven't carried out all our election promises. (admit)
He admitted that they hadn't carried out all their election promises.

LAB SESSION 3 (UNITS 7–9)

Drill 1   Making deductions

– Surely they knew we were coming.
– Well, perhaps they didn't get our letter.
So they might not have known we were coming, then.

– He's a maths teacher, isn't he?
– Well, he did English at university.
So he can't be a maths teacher, then.

– Surely they haven't gone out.
– Well, they're not answering the telephone.
So they must have gone out, then.

Drill 2   Giving reasons for deductions

The lights are on, so they must be at home.
That's right. If they weren't at home, the lights wouldn't be on.

Their car's there, so they can't have left.
That's right. If they had left, their car wouldn't be there.

Drill 3   Effects

Women couldn't get good jobs. Tradition made it difficult.
Tradition made it difficult for women to get good jobs.

Women didn't get promoted. Employers prevented them.
Employers prevented women from getting promoted.

Drill 4   Don't do it

There's no petrol. (try to start the car)
It's no use trying to start the car.

We're nearly there now. (catch a bus)
It's not worth catching a bus.

We wouldn't watch it much, anyway. (buy a new TV)
It's not worth buying a new TV.

Drill 5   Getting it right

– *Do you remember that Chinese restaurant we went to last summer?*
– *It was Japanese.*
Of course, it was a Japanese restaurant we went to, wasn't it?

– *The Andrews recommended it, didn't they?*
– *It was the Browns.*
Of course, it was the Browns who recommended it, wasn't it?

Drill 6   Reported questions

Are you married?
She asked me if I was married.

What are you studying?
She wanted to know what I was studying.

LAB SESSION 4 (UNITS 10–12)

Drill 1   Making wishes

I'm so young.
I wish I wasn't so young.

I can't leave school.
I wish I could leave school.

My parents won't listen to me.
I wish my parents would listen to me.

Drill 2   Regrets and explanations

What a fool I was not to park in the car park.
I wish I'd parked in the car park.

Yes, they took your car away, didn't they?
Exactly. If I'd parked in the car park, they wouldn't have taken my car away.

Drill 3   Did or had done?

I sat down and I read my letters.
When I had sat down I read my letters.

I sat down and the chair collapsed.
When I sat down the chair collapsed.

Drill 4   No sooner...

She picked up her case and immediately the handle broke.
No sooner had she picked up her case than the handle broke.

She got onto the motorway and immediately her car broke down.
No sooner had she got onto the motorway than her car broke down.

Drill 5   Big and small differences

Is May or June hotter in England? (slightly)
June is slightly hotter than May.

Which is cheaper – gold or silver? (considerably)
Silver is considerably cheaper than gold.

Do men live longer than women? (not quite)
Men don't live quite as long as women.

Drill 6   Not what I expected

London was big. I'd expected it to be smaller.
London was bigger than I'd expected it to be.

I'd thought it would be very cold. But it wasn't.
It wasn't as cold as I'd thought it would be.

LAB SESSION 5 (UNITS 13–15)

Drill 1   Getting the order right

Touch a chess piece – decide where to move.
You should decide where to move before you touch a chess piece.

Or in other words ...
You shouldn't touch a chess piece until you've decided where to move.

Drill 2 \ The Passive in describing processes

Well, first we collect the letters from the letter boxes.
First the letters are collected from the letter boxes.

And then we take them to the sorting office.
When they've been collected from the letter boxes, they're taken to the sorting office.

And then we stamp on the postmarks.
When they've been taken to the sorting office, the postmarks are stamped on.

Drill 3 Probabilities

– Do you think a lot of people will be late for work tomorrow?
– Oh yes, this is bound to happen.
A lot of people are bound to be late for work tomorrow.

– What about buses? Will the transport authorities provide extra buses?
– Very unlikely, I'd say.
The transport authorities are very unlikely to provide extra buses.

Drill 4 Conditional predictions

You're sure to get there on time – but you'll have to hurry. (provided)
Provided that you hurry, you're sure to get there on time.

If you want to sell it, you'll have to repair it first. (unless)
Unless you repair it first, you won't sell it.

Drill 5 Headline news

PROMPTS FOR NEWS ITEM 1 :

1 London man / make / strange discovery.
2 Tim Johnson / clean / taxi / when / notice / bag / floor.
3 When / open / bag / find / half / million pounds.
4 He / take / bag / straight / police.
5 Police / try / find / person / leave / bag / taxi.
6 They / talk / several / Mr Johnson's customers.
7 So far / no one / claim / money.
8 If money / not claim / six months / it / go / Mr Johnson.

PROMPTS FOR NEWS ITEM 2 :

1 There / be / more problems / London underground / today.
2 200 people / trap / two hours / this morning / rush hour train.
3 Train / take / people / work / when / stop / between stations.
4 Take / nearly two hours / repair / trouble.
5 20 passengers / take / hospital / suffer / shock.
6 Most / them / later / allow / go home.

⟫→

PROMPTS FOR NEWS ITEM 3 :

1 Police / arrest / owner / video shop / Piccadilly.
2 Martin Weeks / arrest / yesterday.
3 He / charge / sell / illegal video tapes.
4 Tapes / say / illegal copies / *Lost Country*.
5 *Lost Country* / not yet / show / British cinemas.
6 *Lost Country* / break / box-office records / America.
7 4000 illegal copies / film / think / sell / Britain.
8 Mr Weeks / appear / court / Monday.

Acknowledgements

The authors and publishers are grateful to the following for permission to reproduce photographs, illustrations and texts:

The British Tourist Authority (photographs on p. 3); Central Office of Information / Manpower Services Commission Youth Training Scheme (advertisement on p. 12 by Saatchi and Saatchi); Popperfoto (photographs on pp. 13 – top left, 160 – bottom left); John Topham Picture Library (photographs on pp. 13 – top right, 96, 160 – bottom right); Richard and Sally Greenhill (photographs on pp. 13 – bottom left, 29, 36 – top left, right and middle, bottom middle, 45, 50, 137, 159 – right); Homer Sykes (photograph on p. 13 – bottom right); ADAGP and Adelaide de Menil (photograph of *Souvenir de Voyage III* by René Magritte on p. 17, © ADAGP, Paris 1984); A. P. Watt Ltd (adapted extract on p. 21, from *A Dream of Wessex* by Christopher Priest, published by Faber); Nigel Luckhurst (photographs on pp. 34, 43, 48, 52, 53, 116, 117 – bottom right, 126, 127 – top left and right); Sylvester Jacobs (photographs on pp. 36 – bottom left and bottom right, 158 – left, 159 – left); the Kobal Collection (film stills on pp. 40–41); Peter Clarke (cartoons on pp. 50 – top and 51 – bottom, which appeared in *The Guardian*); Trog and *The Observer* (cartoon on p. 50 – bottom); Barnaby's Picture Library (photographs on pp. 51, 54, 75, 127 – bottom, 140, 149 – bottom, 158 – right, 162 – top, 163); Mary Evans Picture Library (illustrations on pp. 58, 160 – top left); Fortean Picture Library (photograph on p. 67); Pan Books (article on p. 70, from *The World Atlas of Mysteries* by Francis Hitching, © Pan Books); John Aldous (photograph on p. 87); Dona Haycraft (photograph on p. 92 – top); Fay Godwin (photographs on pp. 92 – bottom, 111); Sue Adler and *The Observer* (photograph on p. 93); Don Binney (photograph on p. 112); Rolls Royce Motors Ltd (photograph on p. 117 – top left); Austin Rover Group Ltd (photograph on p. 117 – middle left); *Classic and Sportscar* magazine (photograph on p. 117 – bottom left); Guinness Books (photograph on p. 117 – top right); *Slimming* magazine (extract on pp. 120–21); Canon Ltd (illustration on p. 125); Hamlyn Publishing Group Ltd (extract on pp. 140–41 and illustration on p. 142, from *Future World* by Peter Goodwin); Christiane Charillon (drawings by Sempé on pp. 144–7); Camera Press (photograph on p. 149 – top); Ian Stuttard (photograph on p. 154); Barry Lewis / Network (photograph on p. 160 – top right); Stephen Shakeshaft (photograph on p. 161); *Cambridge Evening News* (photograph on p. 162 – bottom).

The illustrations on pp. 4, 5, 24, 25 and 65 were drawn by **Keith Howard**; on pp. 10, 47, 76, 77, 98 and 123 by **Dave Parkins**; on pp. 11, 14, 16, 23, 31, 33, 57, 94, 106, 108, 110, 118 and 128 by **Graham Byfield**; on pp. 19, 117, 124, 129, 130, 131 and 136 by **Chris Evans**; on pp. 26 and 103 by **John Flynn**; on pp. 85, 88, 95 and 150 by **Elivia Savadier**.

Book designed by Peter Ducker MSTD